TEACHER'S PET PUBLICATIONS

LITPLAN TEACHER PACK
for
Holes
based on the book by
Louis Sachar

Written by
Marion B. Hoffman

© 2001 Teacher's Pet Publications
All Rights Reserved

This **LitPlan** on Louis Sachar's **Holes**
has been brought to you by Teacher's Pet Publications, Inc.

Copyright Teacher's Pet Publications 2001

Only the student materials in this unit plan may be reproduced. Pages such as worksheets and study guides may be reproduced for use in the purchaser's classroom. For any additional copyright questions, contact Teacher's Pet Publications.

Table of Contents - Holes

Introduction	6
Unit Objectives	9
Reading Assignment Sheet	10
Unit Outline	11
Study Questions (Short Answer)	15
Quiz/Study Questions (Multiple Choice)	28
Pre-reading Vocabulary Worksheets	53
Lesson One (Introductory Lesson)	67
Nonfiction Assignment Sheet	69
Oral Reading Evaluation Form	70
Writing Assignment #1	72
Writing Assignment #2	84
Writing Assignment #3	100
Writing Evaluation Form	77
Vocabulary Review Activities	98
Extra Writing Assignments/Discussion ?s	90
Unit Tests	103
Unit Resource Materials	133
Vocabulary Resource Materials	155

A Few Notes About The Author--Louis Sachar

Fortunately for us today, we can acquire much biographical information on an author from the Internet. If your students have easy computer access, you might want them to explore sites that tell about Louis Sachar.

For now, a quick Internet exploration for biographical material on the author of **Holes** reveals much about this interesting author of children's books. Louis Sachar (pronounced Sacker) was born in 1954 in East Meadow, New York, moved to Southern California in his youth, and now lives in Austin, Texas.

Sachar briefly attended Antioch College in Ohio and eventually graduated from the University of California at Berkeley in 1976. He is a law school graduate who has passed the bar exam, but he chose a writing profession over a legal one. His first book, **Sideways Stories from Wayside School**, was published just as he began law school. But though he has been a lawyer since 1981, he has devoted himself to writing children's literature instead of a legal career.

His interest in children's literature reportedly began when he became a teachers' aide in an elementary school while he was in college. Not only did he earn three credits for helping out at the school, but the work became his favorite and perhaps most important college course.

But Sachar also began to write because he enjoyed reading. The authors he most enjoyed became his heroes, and he wanted to be like them. Today he especially enjoys Kurt Vonnegut, E. L. Doctorow, J. D. Salinger, Tolstoy, and Dostoevsky.

Sachar reportedly writes alone and doesn't talk about a book until it is finished. Usually he begins with just a kernel of inspiration and over time develops it into a good story. He admits that he frequently suffers from writer's block. Sachar believes that his initial inspiration for **Holes** probably came from the long, hot summers he has spent in Texas. Writing **Holes**, which Sachar considers his "best" book, took a year and a half. The book has been published in many other countries.

Holes has won numerous awards, among them the prestigious Newberry Award, the National Book Award, the **New York Times Book Review** Notable Children's Book of the Year, the ALA Best Book for Young Adults, a **School Library Journal** Best Book of the Year, and the **Publishers Weekly** Best Book of the Year.

Some of Sachar's other works are **Sideways Stories from Wayside School, Johnny's in the Basement, Someday Angeline, Sixth Grade Secrets, There's a Boy in the Girls' Bathroom, The Boy Who Lost His Face, Wayside School is Falling Down, Dogs Don't Tell Jokes,** the Marvin Redpost series **(Marvin Redpost: Kidnapped at Birth?, Marvin Redpost: Is He a Girl?, and Marvin Redpost: Why Pick on Me?), Alone in His Teacher's House, and Wayside School Gets a Little Stranger.**

A Few Notes - **Holes** - page 2

In **Holes**, Sachar has written an ironic, serious, yet often comic novel that appeals to people of all ages. The book features a poor boy with seemingly incredibly bad luck–Stanley Yelnats, whose name "was spelled the same frontward and backward." He is sent to Camp Green Lake, a juvenile detention facility for bad boys that is neither a camp, nor green, nor the site of a lake. In addition, the book is crammed with such colorful characters as Stanley himself; Miss Katherine Barlow, aka Kissin' Kate Barlow, the school teacher turned robber; the sunflower seed spitting Mr. Sir, who talks constantly in Girl Scout allusions; Madame Zeroni, the one-legged gypsy, whose story plays such a central role in the novel; X-Ray; Armpit; the Warden with the red fingernails; Charles "Trout" Walker; Sam the Onion Man whose only real sin was caring deeply for another person; the donkey Mary Lou; and Zero/Hector Zeroni.

Holes is a delightful, enlightening, clever, and satisfying book whose environment is one of lively growth as well as dangerous destruction. Indeed, this book is so full of twists and turns and delightful bits of irony that a person might need to read it more than once, or even twice, in order to glean its total meaning.

Introduction - Holes

This unit has been designed to develop students' reading, writing, thinking, and language skills through exercises and activities related to **Holes** by Louis Sachar. It includes twenty-one lessons, quizzes, worksheets, unit tests, and extra resource materials.

The **introductory lesson** introduces students to one of the novel's main themes (aloneness) through a bulletin board activity. During the novel's introduction, students will learn how the board's activities relate to the book they are beginning to read. Depending on how long you can, or want to, keep the bulletin board intact in the classroom, you might want to keep referring to it to deepen students' thoughts about how easy it is to be totally alone, even when in a group of people.

The eleven **reading assignments** are approximately twenty pages each; some are a little shorter, while others are a little longer. Students have approximately fifteen minutes of pre-reading work to do prior to each reading assignment. This pre-reading work involves reviewing the study questions for the assignment and doing some vocabulary work for the vocabulary words they will encounter in their reading.

The **study guide questions** are fact based: students can find the answers to these questions right in the text. The questions come in two formats: short answer or multiple choice. The best use of these materials is probably to use the short answer version of the questions as study guides for students (since answers will be more complete) and to use the multiple choice version for occasional quizzes.

The **vocabulary work** is intended to enrich students' vocabularies as well as to aid in their understanding of the novel. Prior to each reading assignment, students will complete a two-part worksheet for approximately seven or eight vocabulary words in the upcoming reading assignment. Part I focuses on students' use of general knowledge and contextual clues by giving the sentence in which the word appears in the text. Students may then write down what they think the words mean based on their usage. Part II nails down the definitions of the words by giving students dictionary definitions of them and having students match the words to the correct definitions based on the words' contextual usage. Students should then have an understanding of the words when they meet them in the text.

After each reading assignment, students will go back and formulate answers for the study guide questions. Discussion of these questions will serve as a **review** of the most important events and ideas presented in the reading assignments.

A series of **extra discussion questions** is part of Lesson Twelve. These questions will give students an opportunity to use more critical thinking skills and should provide for some lively class discussions. Feel free to use these questions in whatever way seems most appropriate for your students. If you like, the extra discussion questions can become the basis for some **group activities**. They can be used at any time during your teaching of the novel: there is nothing magical about using them in Lesson Twelve.

Introduction - **Holes** - page 2

The extra discussion questions focus on interpretation, critical analysis, and personal response, employing a variety of thinking skills and adding to the students' understanding of the novel. In fact, if your students enjoy classroom discussions, you might have them come up with additional questions for consideration.

The LitPlan for **Holes** was created to give you lots of flexibility. You may use the plan as a self-contained guide to teaching the novel, but you will also find that it gives you the opportunity to define your classroom approach for yourself. Sometimes students can just work alone in and out of class, sometimes they can work in small groups, sometimes they will be giving and listening to reports, and sometimes the group as a whole will be focused on a classroom assignment or discussion that relies heavily on their participation. Lesson Thirteen, which affords an opportunity to do role playing, and Lesson Nineteen, which offers some vocabulary games the students may play, create an environment for students to work with each other.

After students complete extra discussion questions, there is a **vocabulary review** lesson which pulls together all of the fragmented vocabulary lists for the reading assignments and gives students a review of all of the words they have studied. (Note: **Holes** is a remarkably complex book that is written, for the most part, in a very simple, easy-to-understand way. Depending on your students' skills level, the words might prove not to be especially challenging to them. Should that be the case, you might like to use some of the vocabulary time having students come up with synonyms and antonyms for the vocabulary words. Maybe students could even play with using all vocabulary words from one reading assignment in a sentence. These sentences–some of them perhaps written mostly for fun–could be put on the board prior to class.)

There are three **writing assignments** in this unit, each with the purpose of informing/explaining, expressing personal opinion, or persuading. Through the writing assignments, students will become familiar with a variety of rhetorical devices through which to organize their thoughts. The first writing assignment, introduced in Lesson Six, is to inform/explain, but students will also be defining the word "wasteland" as they write. The second assignment, introduced in Lesson Ten, is to express a personal opinion, but as students write about nicknames, they might very well use classification and some narrative techniques. The third and final writing assignment, introduced in Lesson Nineteen, gives students six different topics on which to write persuasively. By the time that they are in Lesson Nineteen, they should be able to write a satisfactory argument and to utilize various rhetorical methods.

There is also a **nonfiction reading assignment**. Students are required to read some nonfiction related in some way to **Holes.** After reading their nonfiction pieces, students will fill out a worksheet on which they answer questions regarding facts, interpretation, criticism, and personal opinions. Students are also given the opportunity to make **oral presentations** about the nonfiction pieces they have read. This method not only exposes all students to a wealth of information, it also gives students a chance to practice **public speaking**.

Introduction - **Holes** - page 3

There is an optional **class project** (Project Juvenile Detention Centers) through which students gain some additional knowledge of the problems and proffered solutions to juvenile crime in this country. Feel free to use the entire project, to modify it, or to eliminate it altogether. You might even want to use parts of it to create extra credit projects.

Review lessons throughout the plan pull together all of the aspects of the unit. Not only will the reviews help students to connect all the threads of the novel, but they also will give you a clear picture of whether or not students have understood what they have read.

The **unit test** comes in three types: short answer, advanced short answer (more critical thinking), and multiple choice. Altogether there are five unit tests.

There are additional **support materials** throughout the LitPlan–**games**, **puzzles**, **bulletin board ideas**. There are **answer keys** and forms through which to evaluate students' progress. As always, please feel free to use whatever appeals to you and will be supportive of your students' learning.

You are also being provided with two forms–an **Oral Reading Evaluation Form** and a **Writing Evaluation Form**–to use in any way you wish. Both forms may be used by you and/or by the students.

A final note: You know your students, yourself, and your school environment better than anyone else does. This LitPlan is designed to be supportive of you, not to restrict you in your own personal teaching style. The materials in this LitPlan are offered to complement your teaching style and to contribute to your students' optimal learning experience.

Unit Objectives - Holes

1. Through reading and discussing **Holes**, students will preliminarily gain a better understanding of the theme of aloneness and the importance of the individual. Students are also encouraged to consider such themes as bravery, revenge, courage, family values, friendship, greed, and loyalty. And of course **Holes** offers ample material to generate discussions of good vs evil.

2. Students will demonstrate their understanding of the text on four levels: factual, interpretive, critical, and personal.

3. Students will define and, it is hoped, express their own viewpoints on the aforementioned themes.

4. Students will be exposed to several different points of view and will learn something about standing up for one's principles and being true to oneself and to others.

5. Students will learn something about juvenile detention in their town and perhaps in their nation.

6. Students will be given the opportunity to practice reading aloud and silently to improve their skills in each area. They will from time to time receive feedback on their reading ability.

7. Students will answer questions to demonstrate their knowledge and understanding of the main events and characters in **Holes** as they relate to the author's theme development.

8. Students will enrich their vocabularies and improve their understanding of the novel through the vocabulary lessons prepared for use in conjunction with the novel.

9. The writing assignments in this unit are geared to several purposes:
    A. To have students demonstrate their ability to inform/explain, to express personal opinions, and to persuade.
    Note: Students will demonstrate ability to write effectively **to inform/explain** by developing and organizing facts to convey information. Students will demonstrate the ability to write effectively **to express personal opinions** by selecting a form and its appropriate elements. And they will demonstrate the ability to write effectively **to persuade** by selecting and organizing relevant information, establishing an argumentative purpose, and designing an appropriate strategy for a specific audience.
    B. To check the students' reading comprehension
    C. To make students think about the ideas presented by the novel.
    D. To encourage logical thinking

Reading Assignment Sheet - Holes

Date Assigned	Reading Assignment	Completion Date
	pp 3-20	
	pp 21-40	
	pp 41-58	
	pp 59-79	
	pp 80-100	
	pp 101-123	
	pp 127-144	
	pp 145-159	
	pp 160-181	
	pp 182-197	
	pp 198-233	

Unit Outline - Holes

1 Introduction to unit Distribution of materials for unit Bulletin board activity	2 Study ?? 3-20 Vocab 3-20	3 Begin theme discussion Read aloud 3-20 Evaluate reading Study ?? 21-40 Vocab 21-40	4 Review 3-20 Read 21-40 In-class activity (good counselor)	5 Review 21-40 Study ?? 41-58 Vocab 41-58 RA 41-58
6 WA #1	7 Review 41-58 Paragraph writing Study ?? 59-79 Vocab 59-79	8 Read 59-79 Class discussion (Stanley's growth) Study ?? 80-100 Vocab 80-100 RA 80-100	9 Review 80-100 Class discussion (Zero's character development) Prep for NFRA.	10 Begin NFRA Assign WA #2 Study ?? 101-123 Vocab 101-123 RA 101-123
11 Review 101-123 Set up class project Study ??127-144 Vocab 127-144	12 Read 127-144 Review 3-144 Use extra discussion questions	13 Assign study ?? and vocab. 145-159 RA 145-159 Read 160-181 Oral reports NFRA	14 Review 145-159 Study ?? 160-181 RA 160-181 Oral reports NFRA	15 Oral reports NFRA Review 160-181
16 Study ?? 181-197 Vocab 181-197 Catch up on loose ends	17 Read 181-197 Study ?? 198-233 Vocab 198-233 RA 198-233 Begin project reports	18 Continue project reports Make sure everyone understands book	19 Continue project reports Vocabulary review for whole book	20 WA #3
21 Unit Tests				

Key:

    NFRA = Nonfiction Reading Assignment
    RA = Reading Assignment
    WA = Writing Assignment

STUDY GUIDE QUESTIONS

Short Answer Study Questions - Holes

PART ONE

Pages 3-20
1. What is the first revelation of the book? (Hint: it comes in the first sentence.)
2. What is the worst thing that can happen to a person at Camp Green Lake?
3. Who gets sent to Camp Green Lake?
4. Who supposedly is to blame for Stanley's bad luck in being convicted of a crime?
5. Who put a curse on the Yelnats family?
6. What is especially unusual about Stanley Yelnats' name?
7. Who supposedly robbed the stagecoach of the first Stanley Yelnats?
8. Who at the camp has a tattoo of a rattlesnake on his arm?
9. How is Stanley told to remember the name of his counselor?
10. Why does the counselor say Zero is called "Zero"?

Pages 21-40
1. Why didn't Stanley like taking a shower at the camp?
2. What was Clyde Livingston's nickname?
3. What was Stanley's excuse when he was accused of stealing the sneakers?
4. What did Mr. Pendanski say was the reason the boys were digging holes?
5. Who was Myra Menke?
6. What did Myra's father want in exchange for his daughter?
7. What promise did Stanley's great-great-grandfather make to Madame Zeroni?
8. What was the song Madame Zeroni wanted to hear?
9. How did Myra want to choose a husband?
10. What was the most important thing about Sarah Miller?

Pages 41-58
1. What color are the eyes of a yellow-spotted lizard?
2. What did the sign on the camp's rec room say?
3. When Stanley first wrote a letter to his mother, what did he tell her about the camp?
4. What did Stanley first find that he thought might be of interest to the Warden?
5. Why was Stanley glad that the other boys called him "Caveman"?
6. What was the boys' nickname for Mr. Pendanski?

Pages 59-79
1. What was the second thing that Stanley found in a hole?
2. Who did Stanley bring the gold tube to?
3. What color was the Warden's hair?
4. How did the Warden know all of the boys' nicknames?
5. What was Stanley's big revelation about the purpose of the digging?
6. What was Stanley's father trying to invent?

Short Answer Study Questions - **Holes** - page 2

Pages 80-100
1. What did each boy do when he finished digging his hole?
2. What was Stanley's big revelation about Zero?
3. What did Zero ask Stanley to do for him?
4. What was Mr. Sir's favorite expression?
5. Who stole Mr. Sir's sunflower seeds?
6. What did the Warden say was the special ingredient in her red nail polish?
7. What did the Warden do to Mr. Sir in Stanley's presence?
8. Who dug Stanley's hole for him after the sunflower seed incident?
9. What did Stanley suddenly realize about the gold tube he found?

Pages 101-123
1. What special prize did Miss Katherine Barlow win every Fourth of July?
2. What was Miss Barlow's profession in Greek Lake?
3. What did Miss Barlow say when "Trout" Walker invited her to go out in his boat?
4. What did Mr. Sir do to "get back at" Stanley?
5. What special remedy did Sam offer to the people of Green Lake?
6. How did Miss Barlow get Sam to stay near the schoolhouse?
7. Why did the townspeople get so upset when Miss Barlow and Sam kissed?
8. What ultimately happened to Sam?
9. What was Zero's real name?
10. How did Miss Barlow die?

PART TWO AND PART THREE
Pages 127-144
1. What did Stanley think he saw in the rock formation on the mountain peak?
2. What is Stanley's great-grandfather reputed to have said after Kate Barlow robbed him and left him stranded in the desert?
3. What did Zero do in exchange for Stanley's teaching him to read and write?
4. Why did Stanley hit Zigzag?
5. Who attacked Zigzag when he started to beat Stanley?
6. How did the Warden respond to Zero's helping Stanley to dig his holes?
7. What did Zero say when the Warden made her announcement about digging and teaching?
8. What did Zero do when Mr. Pendanski handed him the shovel?
9. What did Zero do after he attacked Mr. Pendanski?
10. What did the Warden, Mr. Pendanski, and Mr. Sir do to cover up Zero's absence?

Short Answer Study Questions - **Holes** - page 3

Pages 145-159
1. What most troubled Stanley's conscience after Zero disappeared?
2. Whenever Stanley thought it was too late to go after Zero, what else would he think?
3. How did Stanley escape from the camp to go after Zero?
4. How much water was in Stanley's canteen when he escaped?
5. What object did Stanley find?
6. Who was hiding under the Mary Lou?
7. What was the "sploosh" that Zero had been drinking?

Pages 160-181
1. Where were Stanley and Zero headed?
2. Who was the original Mary Lou?
3. What worried Stanley most about the possibility of his dying?
4. What signal do Stanley and Zero give each other several times?
5. What was making Zero sick on the climb to Big Thumb?
6. When Stanley dug for water, what did he find?
7. What did Zero confess to Stanley?
8. What three things had Stanley done for Zero when he sang to him?
9. What did Mrs. Tennyson of Green Lake believe cured her daughter Becca?

Pages 182-197
1. What did Zero and Stanley eat to stay alive?
2. After Zero stole the sneakers and wore them for a while, what did he do with them?
3. How did Zero finally get arrested?
4. What finally made Stanley feel happiness?
5. After the feeling of happiness passed, what did Stanley feel?
6. What did Zero reminisce about on the climb down the mountain?
7. When Zero and Stanley got back to Camp Green Lake, what did they do?

Pages 198-233
1. What did Stanley hope to find in the hole that he and Zero searched?
2. How did Zero and Stanley get food and fresh water from the camp?
3. What did Zero and Stanley find in the hole?
4. What happened to spoil their enjoyment of finding the suitcase?
5. What was discovered on the suitcase as Zero held it?
6. While waiting for the lizards to strike, what did the Warden say she would tell the Attorney General?

Short Answer Study Questions - **Holes** - page 4

7. What did Stanley try to think about to keep his mind off the lizards?
8. How were Stanley and Zero finally rescued?
9. What was written on the metal suitcase?
10. Why did Stanley's lawyer say she couldn't help Zero?
11. Why did the lawyer finally say she would help Zero?
12. How did Stanley's lawyer get involved with his case?
13. Who believes that there never was a curse?
14. But what happened the day after Stanley carried Zero up the mountain?
15. What will become of Camp Green Lake?
16. What jewels were in the suitcase Stanley and Zero found?
17. What else was in the suitcase?
18. Approximately how much money did Stanley and Zero each receive?
19. Who was featured on the commercial during the Super Bowl break?
20. What was the name of Stanley's father's invention to cure bad smelling feet?
21. Who was at the Yelnats' party with Zero?
22. What did Zero's mother sing to her son?

Key: Short Answer Study Questions - Holes

PART ONE
Pages 3-20

1. What is the first revelation of the book? (Hint: it comes in the first sentence.)
   The first revelation is that there is no lake at Camp Green Lake.

2. What is the worst thing that can happen to a person at Camp Green Lake?
   The worst thing that can happen is to be bitten by a yellow-spotted lizard.

3. Who gets sent to Camp Green Lake?
   Bad boys get sent to Camp Green Lake.

4. Who supposedly is to blame for Stanley's bad luck in being convicted of a crime?
   Stanley's no-good-dirty-rotten-pig-stealing-great-great-grandfather is to blame.

5. Who put a curse on the Yelnats family?
   A one-legged Gypsy named Madame Zeroni put the curse on the family.

6. What is especially unusual about Stanley Yelnats' name?
   His name is spelled the same frontward and backward.

7. Who supposedly robbed the stagecoach of the first Stanley Yelnats?
   Kissin' Kate Barlow was said to have robbed his stagecoach.

8. Who at the camp has a tattoo of a rattlesnake on his arm?
   Mr. Sir has a tattoo of a rattlesnake on his arm.

9. How is Stanley told to remember the name of his counselor?
   He is told to remember "pen, dance, key" (Pendanski).

10. Why does the counselor say Zero is called "Zero"?
    He says that it's because Zero has nothing inside his head.

Pages 21-40

1. Why didn't Stanley like taking a shower at the camp?
   He didn't like taking a shower because there was only cold water.

2. What was Clyde Livingston's nickname?
   His nickname was "Sweet Feet."

Short Answer Key - **Holes** - page 2

3. What was Stanley's excuse when he was accused of stealing the sneakers?
   He said the sneakers had fallen from the sky and one hit him on the head.

4. What did Mr. Pendanski say was the reason the boys were digging holes?
   He said they were digging holes to build character.

5. Who was Myra Menke?
   She was the girl that Stanley's great-great-grandfather was in love with.

6. What did Myra's father want in exchange for his daughter?
   He wanted the fattest pit that could be offered.

7. What promise did Stanley's great-great-grandfather make to Madame Zeroni?
   He said he would carry her up the mountain, drink from the stream, and sing the song to her.

8. What was the song Madame Zeroni wanted to hear?
   The song was the pig lullaby ("If only, if only...").

9. How did Myra want to choose a husband?
   She wanted to choose the man who picked a number closest to hers between one and ten.

10. What was the most important thing about Sarah Miller?
    She could think for herself.

Pages 41-58

1. What color are the eyes of a yellow-spotted lizard?
   The lizard's eyes are red.

2. What did the sign on the camp's rec room say?
   The sign said, "Wreck Room."

3. When Stanley first wrote a letter to his mother, what did he tell her about the camp?
   He told her everything was okay, just as if he were at a real camp.

4. What did Stanley first find that he thought might be of interest to the Warden?
   He found a fossil.

5. Why was Stanley glad that the other boys called him "Caveman"?
   He was glad because the nickname meant that the boys had accepted him.

Short Answer Key - **Holes** - page 3

6. What was the boys' nickname for Mr. Pendanski?
They nicknamed him "Mom."

Pages 59-79

1. What was the second thing that Stanley found in a hole?
Stanley found a gold tube engraved with a heart and the letters "KB."

2. Who did Stanley bring the gold tube to?
He brought the tube to X-Ray.

3. What color was the Warden's hair?
The Warden's hair was red.

4. How did the Warden know all of the boys' nicknames?
They thought she spied on them through tiny microphones and cameras.

5. What was Stanley's big revelation about the purpose of the digging?
He realized that the boys weren't digging to build character but to find something.

6. What was Stanley's father trying to invent?
He was trying to invent a way to recycle old sneakers.

Pages 80-100

1. What did each boy do when he finished digging his hole?
He spat in it.

2. What was Stanley's big revelation about Zero?
Stanley learned that Zero couldn't read.

3. What did Zero ask Stanley to do for him?
Zero asked Stanley to teach him to read and write.

4. What was Mr. Sir's favorite expression?
He said that Camp Green Lake wasn't a Girl Scout camp.

5. Who stole Mr. Sir's sunflower seeds?
Magnet stole the seeds.

Short Answer Key - **Holes** - page 4

6. What did the Warden say was the special ingredient in her red nail polish?
She said it was rattlesnake venom.

7. What did the Warden do to Mr. Sir in Stanley's presence?
She struck him in the face with her long fingernails.

8. Who dug Stanley's hole for him after the sunflower seed incident?
Zero dug the hole.

9. What did Stanley suddenly realize about the gold tube he found?
He realized that it was half of a lipstick container.

Pages 101-123

1. What special prize did Miss Katherine Barlow win every Fourth of July?
She won a prize for her spiced peaches.

2. What was Miss Barlow's profession in Green Lake?
She was the town's only schoolteacher.

3. What did Miss Barlow say when "Trout" Walker invited her to go out in his boat?
She said, "no."

4. What did Mr. Sir do to "get back at" Stanley?
He poured his water onto the ground instead of into his canteen.

5. What special remedy did Sam offer to the people of Green Lake?
He offered them onions and products made of onions.

6. How did Miss Barlow get Sam to stay near the schoolhouse?
She found repair jobs for him to do.

7. Why did the townspeople get so upset when Miss Barlow and Sam kissed?
They got upset because Miss Barlow was white and Sam was black.

8. What ultimately happened to Sam?
He was shot and killed in the water.

9. What was Zero's real name?
It was Hector Zeroni.

Short Answer Key - **Holes** - page 5

10. How did Miss Barlow die?
    She was bitten by a lizard and died laughing.

PART TWO AND PART THREE
Pages 127-144

1. What did Stanley think he saw in the rock formation on the mountain peak?
   He thought he saw a giant fist, with the thumb sticking straight up.

2. What is Stanley's great-grandfather reputed to have said after Kate Barlow robbed him and left him stranded in the desert?
   He supposedly said, "I found refuge on God's thumb."

3. What did Zero do in exchange for Stanley's teaching him to read and write?
   Zero dug some of Stanley's hole for him each day.

4. Why did Stanley hit Zigzag?
   He hit Zigzag because Mr. Pendanski told him to.

5. Who attacked Zigzag when he started to beat Stanley?
   Zero attacked Zigzag.

6. How did the Warden respond to Zero's helping Stanley to dig his holes?
   She said everyone had to dig his own hole and the reading lessons had to stop.

7. What did Zero say when the Warden made her announcement about digging and teaching?
   He said he refused to dig another hole.

8. What did Zero do when Mr. Pendanski handed him the shovel?
   He hit Mr. Pendanski across the face when the shovel's blade.

9. What did Zero do after he attacked Mr. Pendanski?
   He ran away.

10. What did the Warden, Mr. Pendanski, and Mr. Sir do to cover up Zero's absence?
    They had all records of Zero's presence destroyed.

Short Answer Key - **Holes** - page 6

<u>Pages 145-159</u>

1. What most troubled Stanley's conscience after Zero disappeared?
   Stanley was worried that Zero was still alive and was searching for water.

2. Whenever Stanley thought it was too late to go after Zero, what else would he think?
   Stanley would think, "But what if it wasn't too late?"

3. How did Stanley escape from the camp to go after Zero?
   Stanley stole the water truck, wrecked it, and then simply ran.

4. How much water was in Stanley's canteen when he escaped?
   There was no water in his canteen at all.

5. What object did Stanley find?
   He found Sam's boat, "Mary Lou."

6. Who was hiding under the boat?
   Zero was hiding under the boat.

7. What was the "sploosh" that Zero had been drinking?
   It was hundred-year-old peach nectar.

<u>Pages 160-181</u>

1. Where were Stanley and Zero headed?
   They were headed toward Big Thumb.

2. Who was the original Mary Lou?
   It was Sam's donkey.

3. What worried Stanley most about the possibility of his dying?
   He worried that his parents would never know what had happened to him.

4. What signal do Stanley and Zero give each other several times?
   They give the "thumbs-up" sign.

5. What was making Zero sick on the climb to Big Thumb?
   The hundred-year-old nectar ("sploosh") was making him sick.

Short Answer Key - **Holes** - page 7

6. When Stanley dug for water, what did he find?
   He found an onion.

7. What did Zero confess to Stanley?
   Zero admitted that he had stolen Clyde Livingston's shoes.

8. What three things had Stanley done for Zero when he sang to him?
   Stanley had carried Zero up the mountain, drank the water with him, and sung to him.

9. What did Mrs. Tennyson of Green Lake believe cured her daughter Becca?
   She thought Sam's onion tonic saved her daughter.

Pages 182-197

1. What did Zero and Stanley eat to stay alive?
   They ate onions from the meadow.

2. After Zero stole the sneakers and wore them for a while, what did he do with them?
   He put them on top of a parked car.

3. How did Zero finally get arrested?
   He got caught stealing a new pair of sneakers from a store.

4. What finally made Stanley feel happiness?
   He finally liked himself.

5. After the feeling of happiness passed, what did Stanley feel?
   He felt scared.

6. What did Zero reminisce about on the climb down the mountain?
   He reminisced about the bits and pieces he remembered about his childhood and his mother.

7. When Zero and Stanley got back to Camp Green Lake, what did they do?
   They got into adjacent holes and waited for the camp to fall asleep.

Pages 198-233

1. What did Stanley hope to find in the hole that he and Zero searched?
   He hoped to find Kate Barlow's hidden treasure.

Short Answer Key - **Holes** - page 8

2. How did Zero and Stanley get food and fresh water from the camp?
   Zero went inside and got them.

3. What did Zero and Stanley find in the hole?
   They found a kind of metal suitcase.

4. What happened to spoil their enjoyment of finding the suitcase?
   The Warden, Mr. Pendanski, and Mr. Sir discovered them.

5. What was discovered on the suitcase as Zero held it?
   A bunch of lizards were on the suitcase.

6. While waiting for the lizards to strike, what did the Warden say she would tell the Attorney General?
   The Warden said they would make up a story about Stanley's running away, falling in a hole, and being struck by lizards. She said they wouldn't even need a story about Zero because he didn't exist.

7. What did Stanley try to think about to keep his mind off the lizards?
   He thought about childhood scenes and about his mother.

8. How were Stanley and Zero finally rescued?
   Stanley's lawyer and the Texas Attorney General showed up.

9. What was written on the metal suitcase?
   The name "Stanley Yelnats" was written on the suitcase.

10. Why did Stanley's lawyer say she couldn't help Zero?
    She said she couldn't help Zero because she had no court order to do so.

11. Why did the lawyer finally say she would help Zero?
    She said she would help Zero because there were no records to show why he was incarcerated or for how long.

12. How did Stanley's lawyer get involved with his case?
    She got involved because, as a patent attorney, she was helping Stanley's father with his new product.

Short Answer Key - **Holes** - page 9

13. Who believes that there never was a curse?
    Stanley's mother believes that there never was a curse.

14. But what happened the day after Stanley carried Zero up the mountain?
    Stanley's father invented his cure for foot odor.

15. What will become of Camp Green Lake?
    In a few years it will become a Girl Scout camp.

16. What jewels were in the suitcase Stanley and Zero found?
    The suitcase held jewels of poor quality, worth no more than twenty thousand dollars.

17. What else was in the suitcase?
    The suitcase held stock certificates, deeds of trust, and promissory notes.

18. Approximately how much money did Stanley and Zero each receive?
    Stanley and Zero each received a little less than a million dollars.

19. Who was featured on the commercial during the Super Bowl break?
    Clyde "Sweet Feet" Livingston was featured on the commercial.

20. What was the name of Stanley's father's invention to cure bad smelling feet?
    The product was called "Sploosh."

21. Who was at the Yelnats' party with Zero?
    Zero's mother was at the party.

22. What did Zero's mother sing to her son?
    She sang the lullaby, "If only, if only…"

Multiple Choice Questions - Holes

PART ONE
Pages 3-20

1. What is the first revelation of the book? (Hint: it comes in the first sentence.)
   a. Nobody but Stanley is staying at the camp.
   b. There are girls at the camp.
   c. There is no lake at Camp Green Lake.
   d. The Warden is a man.

2. What is the worst thing that can happen to a person at Camp Green Lake?
   a. To have to go to see the Warden
   b. To have to dig two holes a day
   c. To be bitten by a yellow-spotted lizard
   d. To have all shower privileges taken away

3. Who gets sent to Camp Green Lake?
   a. Pretty girls
   b. Bad boys
   c. Basketball players
   d. Boys whose parents don't like them

4. Who supposedly is to blame for Stanley's bad luck in being convicted of a crime?
   a. His mother
   b. His father
   c. His great-grandfather's friend
   d. His no-good-dirty-rotten-pig-stealing-great-great-grandfather

5. Who put a curse on the Yelnats family?
   a. Mr. Pendanski
   b. The Warden
   c. A one-legged gypsy named Madame Zeroni
   d. Clyde Livingston

6. What is especially unusual about Stanley Yelnats' name?
   a. It is spelled the same frontward and backward.
   b. It has the same number of letters in his first and last names.
   c. It is an alias for his real name, Igor Barkov.
   d. Mr. Sir's brother-in-law has the same name..

Multiple Choice Quizzes - **Holes** 3-20 Continued

6. Who supposedly robbed the stagecoach of the first Stanley Yelnats?
   a. Mr. Pendanski's best friend
   b. Sam the Onion Man
   c. Kissin' Kate Barlow
   d. A one-legged Gypsy

7. Who at the camp has a tattoo of a rattlesnake on his arm?
   a. Mr. Pendanski
   b. The Warden
   c. Magnet
   d. Mr. Sir

8. How is Stanley told to remember the name of his counselor?
   a. Memorize it every day.
   b. Remember that it sounds kind of Polish.
   c. Remember "pen, dance, key."
   d. Write it down.

9. Why does the counselor say Zero is called "Zero"?
   a. Because it rhymes with mirror
   b. Because he failed math in school
   c. Because Zero has nothing inside his head
   d. Because he is a criminal, a zero

Multiple Choice Quizzes - **Holes**
Pages 21-40

1. Why didn't Stanley like taking a shower at the camp?
    a. Because the other boys teased him about being too clean
    b. Because the water got too hot
    c. Because there was no soap available
    d. Because there was only cold water

2. What was Clyde Livingston's nickname?
    a. His nickname was "Tall Boy."
    b. His nickname was "Clydo the Great."
    c. His nickname was "Livingston's Living."
    d. His nickname was "Sweet Feet."

3. What was Stanley's excuse when he was accused of stealing the sneakers?
    a. He said his mother bought them for him.
    b. He said someone gave them to him on the street.
    c. He said the sneakers had fallen from the sky and one hit him on the head.
    d. He said that he blacked out and couldn't remember where the sneakers came from.

4. What did Mr. Pendanski say was the reason the boys were digging holes?
    a. To have a place to bury the lizards
    b. To build character
    c. To make the Warden smile
    d. To get an extra shower in the evening

5. Who was Myra Menke?
    a. Stanley's girlfriend from back home
    b. Madame Zeroni's close friend
    c. The girl that Stanley's great-great-grandfather was in love with
    d. Stanley's mother's best friend

6. What did Myra's father want in exchange for his daughter?
    a. Five hundred dollars
    b. The fattest pig that could be offered
    c. A smart donkey
    d. A person who would sing to him

Multiple Choice Quizzes - **Holes** 21-40 Continued

7. What promise did Stanley's great-great-grandfather make to Madame Zeroni?
    a. That he would never forget her
    b. That he would always be faithful to her
    c. That he would carry her up the mountain, drink from the stream, and sing the song to her
    d. That he would climb all the way up the mountain to see if there was any water there

8. What was the song Madame Zeroni wanted to hear?
    a. The song was the pig lullaby ("If only, if only...").
    b. The song was a popular love song.
    c. The song was one that she had written ("If you care, if you care...).
    d. The song was one that her great-grandfather had taught her.

9. How did Myra want to choose a husband?
    a. She wanted to pick the best singer.
    b. She wanted to pick the best dancer.
    c. She wanted to pick the smartest man.
    d. She wanted to pick the man who chose a number closest to hers between one and ten.

10. What was the most important thing about Sarah Miller?
    a. She was very beautiful.
    b. She could think for herself.
    c. She had a lovely name.
    d. She was very rich.

Multiple Choice Quizzes - **Holes**

Pages 41-58

1. What color are the eyes of a yellow-spotted lizard?
    a. Brown
    b. Red
    c. Blue
    d. Hazel

2. What did the sign on the camp's rec room say?
    a. "Come in and relax"
    b. "Wreck Room"
    c. "Rec Room inside"
    d. "For boys only"

3. When Stanley first wrote a letter to his mother, what did he tell her about the camp?
    a. He said he was scared to death at the camp.
    b. He said he really liked the counselors.
    c. He told her everything was okay, just as if he were at a real camp.
    d. He told her that the other boys all said hello.

4. What did Stanley first find that he thought might be of interest to the Warden?
    a. A pretty pendant
    b. Some pink nail polish
    c. A fossil
    d. Money

5. Why was Stanley glad that the other boys called him "Caveman"?
    a. Because the name made him feel strong
    b. Because he felt like he lived in a cave
    c. Because the nickname meant that the boys had accepted him
    d. Because it was better than being called "Barf Bag"

6. What was the boys' nickname for Mr. Pendanski?
    a. "Zigzag"
    b. "Pretend Warden"
    c. "Mom"
    d. "Dad"

Multiple Choice Quizzes - **Holes**

Pages 59-79

1. What was the second thing that Stanley found in a hole?
    a. A bag full of sunflower seeds
    b. A bunch of old dollar bills
    c. A gold tube engraved with a heart and the letters "KB"
    d. A canteen filled with water

2. Who did Stanley bring the gold tube to?
    a. Mr. Sir
    b. The Warden
    c. X-Ray
    d. Zero

3. What color was the Warden's hair?
    a. Black
    b. Brown
    c. Red
    d. Gray

4. How did the Warden know all of the boys' nicknames?
    a. She memorized them.
    b. She had them all written down in a notebook.
    c. The boys thought she spied on them through tiny microphones and cameras.
    d. She had a chart posted on her wall with all of their nicknames on it.

5. What was Stanley's big revelation about the purpose of the digging?
    a. It actually was kind of fun.
    b. It built character in him.
    c. It was easy after a while.
    d. The boys weren't digging to build character but to find something.

6. What was Stanley's father trying to invent?
    a. A new way to feed pigs
    b. A way to recycle old sneakers
    c. A way to transport pigs to market safely
    d. A way to recycle newspapers

Multiple Choice Quizzes - **Holes**
Pages 80-100

1. What did each boy do when he finished digging his hole?
    a. He screamed.
    b. He spat in it.
    c. He called the Warden to see it.
    d. He said a dirty word under his breath.

2. What was Stanley's big revelation about Zero?
    a. He really was dumb.
    b. He couldn't read.
    c. He should have been sent home months ago.
    d. His mother had been looking for him for months.

3. What did Zero ask Stanley to do for him?
    a. To help him to escape
    b. To help him to kill the warden
    c. To help him to find his mother
    d. To teach him to read and write

4. What was Mr. Sir's favorite expression?
    a. He said that the boys were losers.
    b. He said that Camp Greek Lake wasn't a Girl Scout camp.
    c. He said that the boys were building character every day.
    d. He said that he hated the Warden.

5. Who stole Mr. Sir's sunflower seeds?
    a. Mr. Pendanski
    b. Stanley
    c. Zero
    d. Magnet

6. What did the Warden say was the special ingredient in her red nail polish?
    a. Rattlesnake venom
    b. Varnish
    c. Red food coloring
    d. Lizard blood

Multiple Choice Quizzes - **Holes** 80-100 Continued

7. What did the Warden do to Mr. Sir in Stanley's presence?
   a. She said a nasty word.
   b. She struck him in the face with her long fingernails.
   c. She fired him.
   d. She said he wasn't as smart as Mr. Pendanski.

8. Who dug Stanley's hole for him after the sunflower seed incident?
   a. Mr. Pendanski
   b. Magnet
   c. Zero
   d. All of the boys together

9. What did Stanley suddenly realize about the gold tube he found?
   a. It was very pretty.
   b. It didn't look like a fossil.
   c. It was half of a lipstick container.
   d. It probably wasn't worth much to the Warden.

Multiple Choice Quizzes - **Holes**
Pages 101-123

1. What special prize did Miss Katherine Barlow win every Fourth of July?
    a. A special flag
    b. A huge onion
    c. A prize for her spiced peaches
    d. A prize for being the prettiest woman in town

2. What was Miss Barlow's profession in Green Lake?
    a. She was a dancer.
    b. She was the town's only schoolteacher.
    c. She was a professional thief.
    d. She was a fortune teller.

3. What did Miss Barlow say when "Trout" Walker invited her to go out in his boat?
    a. She said, "Thanks anyway, Mister."
    b. She said, "I think not."
    c. She said, "no."
    d. She said, "sure."

4. What did Mr. Sir do to "get back at" Stanley?
    a. He spit at him.
    b. He wrote a note home to his mother.
    c. He poured his water onto the ground instead of into his canteen.
    d. He drank all of Stanley's water.

5. What special remedy did Sam offer to the people of Green Lake?
    a. Cold compresses
    b. Onions and products made of onions
    c. Peach juice
    d. Special water

6. How did Miss Barlow get Sam to stay near the schoolhouse?
    a. She read stories to him.
    b. She found repair jobs for him to do.
    c. She offered to kiss him.
    d. She let him tutor some students.

Multiple Choice Quizzes - **Holes** 101-123 Continued

7. Why did the townspeople get so upset when Miss Barlow and Sam kissed?
   a. Because now she would get all of the onion products
   b. Because the women were jealous of her
   c. Because he was too young for her
   d. Because she was white and Sam was black

8. What ultimately happened to Sam?
   a. He left town very angry with everyone.
   b. He decided to marry Miss Barlow.
   c. He decided to become a schoolteacher.
   d. He was shot and killed in the water.

9. What was Zero's real name?
   a. Zero Yelnats
   b. Hector Zeroni
   c. Hector Yelnats
   d. Zero Barlow

10. How did Miss Barlow die?
    a. Her boat sank.
    b. She shot herself.
    c. She was killed by Sam.
    d. She was bitten by a lizard and died laughing.

Multiple Choice Quizzes - **Holes**

PART TWO AND PART THREE
Pages 127-144

1. What did Stanley think he saw in the rock formation on the mountain peak?
    a. His mother's face
    b. A giant fist, with the thumb sticking straight up
    c. Zero's face
    d. His great-great-grandfather's pig

2. What is Stanley's great-grandfather reputed to have said after Kate Barlow robbed him and left him stranded in the desert?
    a. "Oh, gosh, I've lost everything!"
    b. "I'll get you back after I climb the mountain."
    c. "I'll never trust a woman again."
    d. "I found refuge on God's thumb."

3. What did Zero do in exchange for Stanley's teaching him to read and write?
    a. Zero recommended Stanley to all of the other boys who couldn't read and write.
    b. Zero said nice things about Stanley to the Warden.
    c. Zero dug some of Stanley's holes for him each day.
    d. Zero promised to write a note to Stanley's parents.

4. Why did Stanley hit Zigzag?
    a. Because he was angry with him
    b. Because Mr. Pendanski told him to
    c. Because he had a hidden violent temper
    d. Because Mr. Sir was watching

5. Who attacked Zigzag when he started to beat Stanley?
    a. Magnet
    b. Mr. Pendanski
    c. Armpit
    d. Zero

6. How did the Warden respond to Zero's helping Stanley to dig his holes?
    a. She thought it was a good idea.
    b. She wished she had thought of it.
    c. She denied both boys their dinner that night.
    d. She said everyone had to dig his own hole and the reading lessons had to stop.

Multiple Choice Quizzes - **Holes** 127-144 Continued

7. What did Zero do when the Warden made her announcement about digging and teaching?
   a. Zero cursed at her.
   b. Zero threatened to run away.
   c. Zero cried.
   d. Zero refused to dig another hole.

8. What did Zero do when Mr. Pendanski handed him the shovel?
   a. He hit Mr. Pendanski across the face with the shovel's blade.
   b. He spit at the Warden.
   c. He threw the shovel at Stanley.
   d. He cried.

9. What did Zero do after he attacked Mr. Pendanski?
   a. He sat down and sobbed.
   b. He went after the Warden with the shovel.
   c. He ran away.
   d. He apologized.

10. What did the Warden, Mr. Pendanski, and Mr. Sir do to cover up Zero's absence?
    a. They laughed.
    b. They had all records of Zero's presence destroyed.
    c. They went looking for him.
    d. They got very frightened because the authorities might come to the camp.

Multiple Choice Quizzes - **Holes**
Pages 145-159

1. What most troubled Stanley's conscience after Zero disappeared?
    a. That Zero might hate him
    b. That Zero might blame him for his problems
    c. That Zero was still alive and was searching for water
    d. That Zero might have learned to read better if he hadn't been digging holes for Stanley.

2. Whenever Stanley thought it was too late to go after Zero, what else would he think?
    a. He would think he himself would have gotten caught if he had gone after Zero.
    b. He would think that finding Zero was really the responsibility of the Warden.
    c. He would think, "But what if it wasn't too late?"
    d. He would be glad that he himself hadn't tried to escape.

3. How did Stanley escape from the camp to go after Zero?
    a. He stole the water truck, wrecked it, and then simply ran.
    b. He ran as fast as he could go.
    c. He pretended to go inside the camp and instead ran off.
    d. He kicked Mr. Sir and Mr. Pendanski and then ran off.

4. How much water was in Stanley's canteen when he escaped?
    a. Only about enough for a day or two
    b. Just a little bit
    c. None
    d. Enough for at least a week

5. What object did Stanley find?
    a. Another huge fossil
    b. Sam's boat, "Mary Lou."
    c. Another lipstick tube
    d. A boat with the name "Kate" on it

6. Who was hiding under the "Mary Lou"?
    a. Mr. Pendanski
    b. Magnet
    c. Zigzag
    d. Zero

7. What was the "sploosh" that Zero had been drinking?
    a. Hundred-year-old onion juice
    b. Old dirty water
    c. Hundred-year-old peach nectar
    d. Carrot juice

Multiple Choice Quizzes - **Holes**
Pages 160-181

1. Where were Stanley and Zero headed?
    a. Toward Big Thumb
    b. Home to their families
    c. Back to the camp
    d. To a place where no one could ever find them

2. Who was the original Mary Lou?
    a. Stanley's great-great-grandfather's first love
    b. Myra Menke's best friend
    c. Kate Barlow's mother
    d. Sam's donkey

3. What worried Stanley most about the possibility of his dying?
    a. He didn't know where he would be buried.
    b. He worried that his parents would never know what happened to him.
    c. He worried that he would be buried in the hole containing the treasure.
    d. He worried that Zero would have to dig the hole for him.

4. What signal do Stanley and Zero give each other several times?
    a. A silly grin
    b. The "V" for victory sign
    c. The "thumbs-up" sign
    d. A word in Morse Code

5. What was making Zero sick on the climb to Big Thumb?
    a. The hundred-year-old nectar ("sploosh")
    b. Anxiety over what he had done back at the camp
    c. Worry that Stanley would die
    d. His conscience

6. When Stanley dug for water, what did he find?
    a. More sploosh
    b. A onion
    c. Sunflower seeds
    d. Another lipstick tube

Multiple Choice Quizzes - **Holes** 160-181 Continued

7. What did Zero confess to Stanley?
    a. Zero said that he really could read and write.
    b. Zero admitted that he had stolen Clyde Livingston's shoes.
    c. Zero said that he had never really liked Stanley.
    d. Zero said that Armpit was really his brother.

8. What three things had Stanley done for Zero when he sang to him?
    a. Carried him up the mountain, drank the water with him, and sung to him
    b. Taught him to read, to write, and to do math better
    c. Taught him how to recognize his own name, how to write it, and how to pronounce it correctly
    d. How to dig holes, how to control his temper, and how to read and write

9. What did Mrs. Tennyson of Green Lake believe cured her daughter Becca?
    a. Flu shots
    b. The town doctor
    c. Sam's onion tonic
    d. Lots of peach nectar

Multiple Choice Quizzes - **Holes**

Pages 182-197

1. What did Zero and Stanley eat to stay alive?
    a. Fish from a stream
    b. Sunflower seeds
    c. Peaches
    d. Onions from the meadow

2. After Zero stole the sneakers and wore them for a while, what did he do with them?
    a. He put them on top of a parked car.
    b. He gave them to an old homeless person.
    c. He returned them to the shelter.
    d. He threw them away in a dumpster.

3. How did Zero finally get arrested?
    a. He tried to retrieve the sneakers from the trash.
    b. Someone told a police officer that they saw Zero with the shoes.
    c. He got caught stealing a new pair of sneakers from a store.
    d. He turned himself in to the police.

4. What finally made Stanley feel happiness?
    a. He felt good about rescuing Zero.
    b. He finally had plenty to eat.
    c. He finally liked himself.
    d. Zero made him laugh at a really funny joke.

5. After the feeling of happiness passed, what did Stanley feel?
    a. He felt silly about being so happy.
    b. He felt very confused about where he and Zero were.
    c. He felt lucky.
    d. He felt scared.

6. What did Zero reminisce about on the climb down the mountain?
    a. About bits and pieces he remembered from his childhood and about his mother
    b. About how silly it was to believe in a curse
    c. About his special days at Camp Green Lake
    d. About how he had attended a baseball game with his father

7. When Zero and Stanley got back to Camp Green Lake, what did they do?
    a. They shouted for someone to come out and see them.
    b. They hollered for Mr. Sir to come outside.
    c. They threatened to kill the Warden.
    d. They got into adjacent holes and waited for the camp to fall asleep.

Multiple Choice Quizzes - **Holes**
Pages 198-233

1. What did Stanley hope to find in the hole that he and Zero searched?
    a. Another fossil
    b. A prettier lipstick tube
    c. Kate Barlow's hidden treasure
    d. More onions

2. How did Zero and Stanley get food and fresh water from the camp?
    a. They forced Magnet to bring some food and water outside.
    b. Stanley went inside and found them.
    c. Mr. Pendanski brought some outside for them.
    d. Zero went inside and got them.

3. What did Zero and Stanley find in the hole?
    a. Onions
    b. Peaches
    c. Sunflower seeds
    d. A kind of metal suitcase

4. What happened to spoil their enjoyment of finding the suitcase?
    a. The suitcase turned out to be empty.
    b. Mr. Warden, Mr. Pendanski, and Mr. Sir discovered them.
    c. Zigzag and Armpit came outside and stole the suitcase.
    d. Stanley got cold feet and decided to put the suitcase back in the hole.

5. What was discovered on the suitcase as Zero held it?
    a. Zero's name
    b. The Warden's name: Mrs. Walker
    c. A bunch of lizards
    d. A big hole

6. While waiting for the lizards to strike, what did the Warden say she would tell the Attorney General?
    a. She said they would claim neither Stanley nor Zero had ever been at the camp.
    b. She said they would make up a story about Stanley's running away, falling in a hole, and being struck by lizards. They wouldn't even need a story about Zero because he didn't exist.
    c. She said they would claim that both Stanley and Zero were mentally ill.
    d. She said they would claim that the boys had stolen the suitcase from her room.

Multiple Choice Quizzes - **Holes** 198-233 Continued

7. What did Stanley try to think about to keep his mind off the lizards?
    a. About childhood scenes and about his mother
    b. About his first big baseball game
    c. About how he wouldn't have to take any more cold showers
    d. About how he used to be bullied in school

8. How were Stanley and Zero finally rescued?
    a. Stanley's parents showed up.
    b. Zero's mother sent a telegram asking for information.
    c. Mr. Pendanski decided to help them to escape.
    d. Stanley's lawyer and the Texas Attorney General showed up.

9. What was written on the metal suitcase?
    a. The Warden's name
    b. Zero's mother's maiden name
    c. The name "Stanley Yelnats"
    d. "Property of Camp Green Lake"

10. Why did Stanley's lawyer say she couldn't help Zero?
    a. Because Zero actually committed a crime
    b. Because Zero's parents hadn't come forward to help
    c. Because Zero couldn't read and write
    d. Because she had no court order to do so

11. Why did the lawyer finally say she would help Zero?
    a. Because she felt sorry for him
    b. Because the Attorney General authorized her to do so
    c. Because there were no records to show why he was incarcerated or for how long
    d. Because she was afraid to leave him behind

12. How did Stanley's lawyer get involved with his case?
    a. She knew a court reporter who told her about his case.
    b. As a patent attorney, she was helping Stanley's father with his new product.
    c. She had investigated Camp Green Lake years before and had decided to check on incarcerated boys to see how they were being treated now.
    d. She got involved at the request of the Texas Attorney General's Office.

Multiple Choice Quizzes - **Holes** 198-233 Continued

13. Who believes that there never was a curse?
    a. The Warden
    b. Zero
    c. Stanley's mother
    d. Stanley's lawyer

14. But what happened the day after Stanley carried Zero up the mountain?
    a. Stanley's father invented his cure for foot odor.
    b. Clyde Livingston invited Stanley to a big baseball game.
    c. Stanley's lawyer saw Clyde Livingston on a television commercial.
    d. A pig was seen in the Yelnats' back yard.

15. What will become of Camp Green Lake?
    a. It will be closed and bulldozed.
    b. It will be used as a place for rookie baseball players to train.
    c. It will be used as a minimum security prison for men.
    d. It will become a Girl Scout camp.

16. What jewels were in the suitcase Stanley and Zero found?
    a. Jewels of poor quality, worth no more than twenty thousand dollars
    b. Many uncut diamonds
    c. Emeralds
    d. Rubies

17. What else was in the suitcase?
    a. Many hundred dollar bills
    b. Letters
    c. A confession from Kate Barlow
    d. Stock certificates, deeds of trust, and promissory notes

18. Approximately how much money did Stanley and Zero each receive?
    a. About fifty thousand dollars
    b. Nearly seventy-five thousand dollars
    c. Only about thirty thousand dollars
    d. A little less than a million dollars

Multiple Choice Quizzes - **Holes** 198-233 Continued

19. Who was featured on the commercial during the Super Bowl break?
    a. A black man advertising onions
    b. A pretty woman demonstrating ways to cook peaches
    c. Clyde "Sweet Feet" Livingston
    d. Stanley's lawyer

20. What was the name of Stanley's father's invention to cure bad smelling feet?
    a. "Sweet Feet"
    b. "Peachy Smell"
    c. "Sploosh"
    d. "Zero's Revenge"

21. Who was at the Yelnats' party with Zero?
    a. His father
    b. His newly-appointed lawyer
    c. His half-brother
    d. His mother

22. What did Zero's mother sing to her son?
    a. A pop tune that Zero especially liked
    b. A song that Stanley wrote for her
    c. The lullaby, "If only, if only..."
    d. A song about a boy wrongly sent to a camp for bad boys

Key - Multiple Choice Quizzes
Holes

PART ONE

Pages 3-20	Pages 21-40	Pages 41-58	Pages 59-79
1. c	1. d	1. b	1. c
2. c	2. d	2. b	2. c
3. b	3. c	3. c	3. c
4. d	4. b	4. c	4. c
5. c	5. c	5. c	5. d
6. c	6. b	6. c	6. b
7. d	7. c		
8. c	8. a		
9. c	9. d		
	10. b		

Pages 80-100	Pages 101-103
1. b	1. c
2. b	2. b
3. d	3. c
4. b	4. c
5. d	5. b
6. a	6. b
7. b	7. d
8. c	8. d
9. c	9. b
	10. d

PART TWO AND PART THREE

Pages 127-144	Pages 145-159	Pages 160-181	Pages 182-197
1. b	1. c	1. a	1. d
2. d	2. c	2. d	2. a
3. c	3. a	3. b	3. c
4. b	4. c	4. c	4. c
5. d	5. b	5. a	5. d
6. d	6. d	6. b	6. a
7. d	7. c	7. b	7. d
8. a		8. a	
9. c		9. c	
10. b			

Key to Multiple Choice Quizzes - **Holes** - page 2

<u>Pages 198-233</u>

1. c
2. d
3. d
4. b
5. c
6. b
7. a
8. d
9. c
10. d
11. c
12. b
13. c
14. a
15. d
16. a
17. d
18. d
19. c
20. c
21. d
22. c

PRE-READING VOCABULARY WORKSHEETS

Vocabulary - Holes

PART ONE
Pages 3-20: Part I: Using Prior Knowledge and Contextual Clues. Below are the sentences in which the vocabulary words appear in the text. Read the sentence. Use any clues you can find in the sentence combined with your prior knowledge, and write what you think the underlined words mean.

1. Now it is just a dry, flat **wasteland**.

2. During the summer the daytime temperature **hovers** around ninety-five degrees in the shade–if you can find any shade.

3. Here's a good rule to remember about rattlesnakes and **scorpions**: If you don't bother them, they won't bother you.

4. The bus wasn't air-conditioned, and the hot, heavy air was almost as **stifling** as the handcuffs.

5. Mrs. Bell wrote the **ratio** on the board, 3:1, unaware of how much embarrassment she had caused both of them.

6. Supposedly, he had a great-great-grandfather who had stolen a pig from a one-legged Gypsy, and she put a curse on him and all his **descendants**.

7. Stanley's father was smart and had a lot of **perseverance**.

8. The land was barren and **desolate**.

Part II: Determining the Meaning
Match the vocabulary words to their dictionary definitions.

___ 1. wasteland   A. dreary, unfit for habitation or use
___ 2. hovers   B. spider-like, definitely venomous
___ 3. scorpion   C. opposite of ancestors
___ 4. stifling   D. not giving up
___ 5. ratio   E. uncultivated or desolate country
___ 6. descendants   F. relation between two things
___ 7. perseverance   G. floats or is suspended in air
___ 8. desolate   H. smothering, suffocating

Vocabulary - **Holes** - page 2

Pages 21-40: Part I: Using Prior Knowledge and Contextual Clues. Below are sentences in which the vocabulary words appear in the text. Read the sentence. Use any clues you can find in the sentence combined with your prior knowledge, and write what you think the underlined words mean.

1. Because of the **scarcity** of water, each camper was only allowed a four-minute shower.

2. Back at school, a bully named Derrick Dunne used to **torment** Stanley.

3. By the time Stanley **retrieved** it, he had missed the bus and had to walk home.

4. Maybe he was in a hurry to bring the shoes to his father, or maybe he was trying to run away from his miserable and **humiliating** day at school.

5. The judge called Stanley's crime **despicable**.

6. He wondered if he had a **defective** shovel.

7. Madame Zeroni warned that if he failed to do this, he and his descendants would be **doomed** for all of eternity.

8. "That's **preposterous**!" exclaimed Igor, expelling saliva as he spoke.

Part II: Determining the Meaning
Match the vocabulary words to their dictionary definitions.

___ 9. scarcity   A. absurd, ridiculous
___ 10. torment   B. being disgraced
___ 11. retrieved   C. condemned to severe penalty
___ 12. humiliating   D. vile, awful
___ 13. despicable   E. shortage
___ 14. defective   F. great pain or anguish
___ 15. doomed   G. flawed, subnormal
___ 16. preposterous   H. got back, regained

Vocabulary - **Holes** - page 3

Pages 41-58: Part I: Using Prior Knowledge and Contextual Clues. Below are sentences in which the vocabulary words appear in the text. Read the sentence. Use any clues you can find in the sentence combined with your prior knowledge, and write what you think the underlined words mean.

1. A lot of people don't believe in **curses**.

2. The water ran out under the walls and **evaporated** quickly in the sun.

3. Even the people looked broken, with their worn-out bodies **sprawled** over the various chairs and sofas.

4. Stanley slipped it back into the **stationery** box.

5. He looked at the **barren** land all around him.

6. Stanley saw his **fossil** being passed around.

7. "It's **pig latin** for Rex [X-Ray]...."

Part II: Determining the Meaning
Match the vocabulary words to their dictionary definitions.

___17. curses	A. converted or changed into a vapor
___18. evaporated	B. sterile, dull, unfruitful
___19. sprawled	C. remnant or trace of an organism of a past geological age (skeleton or leap imprint) embedded in the earth's crust
___20. stationery	D. jargon formed by putting first consonant at the end of a word and adding a syllable (igpay atinlay for pig latin)
___21. barren	E. appeals for evil or injury to befall someone or something
___22. pig latin	F. spread out in straggling or disordered fashion
___23. fossil	G. writing paper and envelopes

Note: According to the dictionary, **pig Latin** should be spelled with a capital **L**.

Vocabulary - **Holes** - page 4

Pages 59-79: Part I: Using Prior Knowledge and Contextual Clues. Below are sentences in which the vocabulary words appear in the text. Read the sentence. Use any clues you can find in the sentence combined with your prior knowledge, and write what you think the underlined words mean.

1. He felt something hard and **metallic**.

2. He looked again at the design **engraved** into the flat bottom of the tube.

3. He could explain the situation to the Warden, and the Warden might make up an excuse for giving him the day off, so X-Ray wouldn't **suspect**.

4. They were only visible for a short while and would soon disappear behind the **haze** of heat and dirt.

5. She gently shook the canteen, letting the water **swish** inside the plastic container.

6. Zero will dig it out of the hole, and Caveman will carefully shovel it into a **wheelbarrow**.

7. It seemed so **familiar**, but he just couldn't place it.

8. Stanley was **amazed**.

Part II: Determining the Meaning
Match the vocabulary words to their dictionary definitions.

___24. metallic   A. filled with surprise, astonished
___25. engraved   B. often encountered, known
___26. suspect   C. to move with a whistle or hiss
___27. haze   D. vehicle with handles, used to convey loads by hand
___28. swish   E. like or containing a metal
___29. wheelbarrow   F. carved, cut, etched into something
___30. familiar   G. have doubts about, distrust
___31. amazed   H. atmospheric moisture, dust, vapor, suspended in air

Vocabulary - **Holes** - page 5

Pages 80-100: Part I: Using Prior Knowledge and Contextual Clues. Below are sentences in which the vocabulary words appear in the text. Read the sentence. Use any clues you can find in the sentence combined with your prior knowledge, and write what you think the underlined words mean.

1. If he jerked too quickly, he felt a **throbbing** pain above his neck where Zigzag's shovel had hit him.

2. His muscles had strengthened, and his hands were tough and **callused**.

3. And as the truck bounced along the dirt, he was able to **appreciate** the air blowing through the open window onto his hot and sweaty face.

4. Stanley wondered if this was how a **condemned** man felt on his way to the electric chair–appreciating all of the good things in life for the last time.

5. He felt nothing but **dread** now.

6. "Do you want to know my secret **ingredient**?"

7. "Rattlesnake **venom**."

8. His body **writhed** in agony.

Part II: Determining the Meaning
Match the vocabulary words to their dictionary definitions.

___32. throbbing   A. twisted, squirmed
___33. callused   B. found guilty
___34. appreciate   C. poisonous secretion of an animal, such as a spider or a snake
___35. condemned   D. beating rapidly or violently; pounding
___36. dread   E. having thickening and hardness of a layer of skin
___37. ingredient   F. in terror of, anticipated with fear, alarm, reluctance
___38. venom   G. value
___39. writhed   H. something that is an element, a part, of

Vocabulary - **Holes** - page 6

Pages 101-123: Part I: Using Prior Knowledge and Contextual Clues. Below are sentences in which the vocabulary words appear in the text. Read the sentence. Use any clues you can find in the sentence combined with your prior knowledge, and write what you think the underlined words mean.

1. A special prize was given every year to Miss Katherine Barlow for her **fabulous** spiced peaches.

2. It made a horrible loud noise and **spewed** ugly black smoke over the beautiful lake.

3. No one even dared to look at his **grotesque** face.

4. Stanley stared at the dark spot on the ground, which quickly **shrank** before his eyes.

5. They would get regular medicine from Doc Hawthorn and onion **concoctions** from Sam.

6. "Just calm your pretty self down a second," the sheriff said in a slow **drawl**.

7. She ran down to the lakefront, where Sam was **hitching** Mary Lou to the onion cart.

8. "You've got exactly ten seconds to tell me where you've hidden your **loot**," said Trout.

Part II: Determining the Meaning
Match the vocabulary words to their dictionary definitions.

___40. fabulous   A. outlandish, bizarre
___41. spewed   B. got smaller
___42. grotesque   C. speech characterized by lengthened, drawn-out vowels
___43. shrank   D. forced out
___44. concoctions   E. stolen goods
___45. drawl   F. hooking to, connecting
___46. hitching   G. barely believable, astonishing
___47. loot   H. preparations made by mixing ingredients

Vocabulary - **Holes** - page 7

PART TWO AND PART THREE

Pages 127-144: Part I: Using Prior Knowledge and Contextual Clues. Below are sentences in which the vocabulary words appear in the text. Read the sentence. Use any clues you can find in the sentence combined with your prior knowledge, and write what you think the underlined words mean.

1. The only time they were **visible** was just at sunup, before the air became hazy.

2. But the **image** of the fist and thumb remained in Stanley's head.

3. He always felt **awkward** while Zero was digging his hole, unsure of what to do with himself.

4. Stanley made a **feeble** attempt to punch Zigzag, then he felt a flurry of fists against his head and neck.

5. If Mr. Pendanski only thought about it, he'd realize it was very **logical** for Zero to think that the letter "h" made the "ch" sound.

6. "He can't go anywhere. The last thing we need is an **investigation**."

7. And even if they did find **refuge** on Big Thumb, he thought, they'd still have to come back here, eventually.

8. For some reason his great-grandfather had felt the **urge** to climb to the top of that mountain.

Part II: Determining the Meaning
Match the vocabulary words to their dictionary definitions.

___48. visible   A. protection or shelter
___49. image   B. systematic examination
___50. awkward   C. lacking strength
___51. feeble   D. clumsy, unskillful
___52. logical   E. able to be seen
___53. investigation   F. reproduction of the form of someone or something
___54. refuge   G. consistent in reasoning
___55. urge   H. force moving one to do something

Vocabulary - **Holes** - page 8

<u>Pages 145-159</u>: Part I: Using Prior Knowledge and Contextual Clues. Below are sentences in which the vocabulary words appear in the text. Read the sentence. Use any clues you can find in the sentence combined with your prior knowledge, and write what you think the underlined words mean.

1. The next morning, out on the lake, Stanley listened as Mr. Sir told Twitch the **requirements** for his hole: "...as wide and as deep as your shovel."

2. He lay on the dirt staring at the truck, which stuck **lopsided** into the ground.

3. The encounter with the lizards had made him very **cautious**.

4. It was a **mirage** caused by the shimmering waves of heat rising off the dry ground.

5. But he could make it to the **mysterious** object.

6. There were enough cracks and holes in the bottom of the boat, now the roof, to provide light and **ventilation**.

7. It was a warm, bubbly, mushy **nectar**, sweet and tangy.

8. It felt like heaven as it flowed over his dry mouth and down his **parched** throat.

Part II: Determining the Meaning
Match the vocabulary words to their dictionary definitions.

___56. requirements   A. something illusory, deceptive
___57. lopsided   B. not fully understood
___58. cautious   C. careful
___59. mirage   D. delicious, invigorating drink
___60. mysterious   E. heavier, larger on one side than on the other
___61. ventilation   F. very dry
___62. nectar   G. necessary things
___63. parched   H. admitting fresh air to replace stale air

Vocabulary - **Holes** - page 9

Pages 160-181: Part I: Using Prior Knowledge and Contextual Clues. Below are sentences in which the vocabulary words appear in the text. Read the sentence. Use any clues you can find in the sentence combined with your prior knowledge, and write what you think the underlined words mean.

1. He was weak and **exhausted**, yet as bad as he felt, he knew that Zero felt ten times worse.

2. He was able to lift Zero high enough for him to grab the **protruding** slab of rock.

3. When they reached flat ground, Stanley looked up to see the sun, a **fiery** ball balancing on top of Big Thumb.

4. As the ground flattened, a huge stone **precipice** rose up ahead of him, just barely visible in the moonlight.

5. Zero's head knocked against the back of his shoulder as he fell and tumbled into a small muddy **gully**.

6. Using both hands, he dug a hole in the **soggy** soil.

7. It took a moment for Stanley to **comprehend**.

8. Zero was **delirious**.

Part II: Determining the Meaning
Match the vocabulary words to their dictionary definitions.

___64. exhausted   A. mentally confused
___65. protruding   B. extremely steep or overhanging mass of rock
___66. fiery   C. very tired, weary
___67. precipice   D. deep ditch cut in the earth by running water
___68. gully   E. saturated, soaked with moisture
___69. soggy   F. very hot
___70. comprehend   G. sticking, jutting out
___71. delirious   H. understand

Vocabulary - **Holes** - page 10

Pages 182-197: Part I: Using Prior Knowledge and Contextual Clues. Below are sentences in which the vocabulary words appear in the text. Read the sentence. Use any clues you can find in the sentence combined with your prior knowledge, and write what you think the underlined words mean.

1. Zero's condition continued to **improve**.

2. It was like a giant **sundial**.

3. But Stanley's trial kept getting **delayed** because of baseball.

4. It would mean living the rest of his life as a **fugitive**.

5. Instead he tried to recapture the feelings he'd had the night before–the **inexplicable** feeling of happiness, the sense of destiny.

6. The onions had **protected** them, like Styrofoam packing material.

7. He waited until he was **certain** the last of the campers had finished for the day.

8. They climbed down into **adjacent** holes, and waited for the camp to fall asleep.

Part II: Determining the Meaning
Match the vocabulary words to their dictionary definitions.

___72. improve   A. put off until another time
___73. sundial   B. not able to be explained or interpreted
___74. delayed   C. get better
___75. fugitive   D. instrument that indicates local solar time
___76. inexplicable   E. kept safe, guarded
___77. protected   F. sure
___78. certain   G. close together, next to
___79. adjacent   H. person running away from the law

Vocabulary - **Holes** - page 11

Pages 198-233: Part I: Using Prior Knowledge and Contextual Clues. Below are sentences in which the vocabulary words appear in the text. Read the sentence. Use any clues you can find in the sentence combined with your prior knowledge, and write what you think the underlined words mean.

1. As his tunnel grew deeper and wider–and more **precarious**–Stanley was able to feel latches on one end of the box, and then a leather handle.

2. He did not **flinch**.

3. "How do I know it's **legitimate**? The boys in my custody have proven themselves dangerous to society. Am I supposed to just turn them loose any time someone hands me a piece of paper?"

4. "He is no longer under your **jurisdiction**," said Stanley's lawyer.

5. "He was obviously **incarcerated** for a reason."

6. Stanley's mother **insists** that there never was a curse.

7. But those changes are **subtle** and hard to measure.

8. Even the contents of the suitcase turned out to be somewhat **tedious**.

Part II: Determining the Meaning
Match the vocabulary words to their dictionary definitions.

___80. precarious   A. shut in, confined, usually in jail
___81. flinch   B. dangerously lacking in security or stability
___82. legitimate   C. tiresome, wearisome
___83. jurisdiction   D. so slight as to be difficult to distinguish
___84. incarcerated   E. refuses to yield
___85. insists   F. draw away from something surprising or painful
___86. subtle   G. lawful, legal
___87. tedious   H. area of authority or control

Key: Vocabulary Worksheets - Holes

PART ONE

Pages 3-20	Pages 21-40	Pages 41-58	Pages 59-79
1. e	9. e	17. e	24. e
2. g	10. f	18. a	25. f
3. b	11. h	19. f	26. g
4. h	12. b	20. g	27. h
5. f	13. d	21. b	28. c
6. c	14. g	22. d	29. d
7. d	15. c	23. c	30. b
8. a	16. a		31. a

Pages 80-100	Pages 101-123
32. d	40. g
33. e	41. d
34. g	42. a
35. b	43. b
36. f	44. h
37. h	45. c
38. c	46. f
39. a	47. e

PART TWO AND PART THREE

Pages 127-144	Pages 145-159	Pages 160-181	Pages 182-197
48. e	56. g	64. c	72. c
49. f	57. e	65. g	73. d
50. d	58. c	66. f	74. a
51. c	59. a	67. b	75. h
52. g	60. b	68. d	76. b
53. b	61. h	69. e	77. e
54. a	62. d	70. h	78. f
55. h	63. f	71. a	79. g

Pages 198-233	
80. b	84. a
81. f	85. e
82. g	86. d
83. h	87. c

DAILY LESSONS

Lesson One

Objectives
1. To introduce the unit on **Holes**
2. To distribute books and other related materials (study guides, reading assignments, etc.)
3. To prepare students to discover the concept of aloneness via a bulletin board activity
4. To prepare a bulletin board activity demonstrating aloneness

Activity #1
Explain briefly to the students why you have chosen **Holes** as a book for them to read. Try to make them understand why you think they will enjoy and learn from the book and the characters and experiences in it.

Activity #2
Distribute the materials students will use in this unit. Explain in detail how students are to use the materials.

Study Guides Students should read the study guide questions for each reading assignment before beginning the assignment to get a feel for what events and ideas are important in the section they are about to read. After reading the section, students will (as a class or individually) answer the questions to review the important events and ideas from that section of the book. Students should keep the study guides as study materials for the unit test.

Vocabulary As they are reading a section of the text, students will do vocabulary work related to the section they are reading. If they hunt for the vocabulary words as they read, students should be able to figure out the contextual meaning of the words. Following the completion of the reading of the book, there will be a vocabulary review of all the words used in the vocabulary assignments. Students should keep their vocabulary work as study materials for the unit test.

Reading Assignment Sheet You need to fill in the reading assignment sheet to let students know when their reading has to be completed. You can either write the assignment on a side chalk board or bulletin board and leave it there for students to see each day, or you can make copies for each student to have. In any case, advise students to become very familiar with the reading assignments so they know what is expected of them.

Extra Activities Center The Unit Resource portion of this unit contains suggestions for a library of related books and articles in your classroom as well as crossword and word search puzzles. Make a center in your room where you will keep these materials for students to use. (Bring the books and articles in from the library and keep several copies of the puzzles on hand.) Explain to students that these materials are available for their use when they finish reading assignments or other class work early.

Lesson #1 - **Holes** - page 2

Nonfiction Assignment Sheet Explain to students that they each are to read at least one nonfiction piece from the in-class library or elsewhere at some time during the unit. They might want to take a book out of the school library (if such books are available for circulation), use a book in the school library, use a book in a local community library, or refer to books that they already have in their homes. Students will fill out a nonfiction assignment sheet after completing the reading to help you evaluate their reading experiences and to help the students to think about and evaluate their own reading.

Books Each school has its own rules and regulations regarding student use of school books. Advise students of the procedures that are usual for your school.

Activity #3
Ask students to think of a time when they felt completely alone. For the next class meeting, they may present a hand-drawn picture of how they felt when alone, bring a cut-out picture from a magazine or newspaper which depicts how they felt, or present a poem or a couple of paragraphs explaining their aloneness. The point is not to create great works of art but instead to get students to thinking of aloneness as Stanley Yelnats, the hero of **Holes** experiences it. If you get some interesting expressions, you might like to post them on the bulletin board–with or without names. If you don't get pictures or writing appropriate to put on the bulletin board, you might bring in a few pictures yourself.

Activity #4
You will want to set the bulletin board up in such a way that students will have occasion to look at it each day that they are reading the novel.

Nonfiction Assignment Sheet - Holes
(To be completed after reading the required nonfiction article)

Name _____ Date _____ Class _____

Title of Nonfiction Read _____

Author _____ Publication Date _____

I. **Factual Summary**: Write a short summary of the piece you read.

II. **Vocabulary**:
    1. Which vocabulary words were difficult?

    2. What did you do to help yourself understand the words?

III. **Interpretation**: What was the main point the author wanted you to get from reading his or her work?

IV. **Criticism**:
    1. Which points of the piece did you agree with or find easy to believe? Why?

    2. Which points did you disagree with or find hard to believe? Why?

V. **Personal Response**:
    1. What do you think about this piece of writing overall?

    2. How does this piece help you better understand the book, **Holes**?

Oral Reading Evaluation - Holes

Name _____ Class _____ Date _____

SKILL	EXCELLENT	GOOD	AVERAGE	FAIR	POOR
Fluency	5	4	3	2	1
Clarity	5	4	3	2	1
Audibility	5	4	3	2	1
Pronunciation	5	4	3	2	1
_____	5	4	3	2	1
_____	5	4	3	2	1

Total _____   Grade _____

Comments:

Lesson Two

Objectives
1. To preview the study questions for PART ONE: pp 3-20
2. To familiarize students with the vocabulary for pp 3-20

Activity #1
Preview the study questions and have students look over the vocabulary words for pp 3-20 of **Holes**. If students do not finish this assignment during the class period, they should complete it, including the vocabulary worksheets, prior to the next class meeting.

Activity #2
Spend a brief time making sure that students have become familiar with the vocabulary words for pp 3-20.

Lesson Three

Objectives
1. To begin consideration and discussion of one theme in **Holes**, namely life as a physical and spiritual wasteland
2. To read pp 3-20 aloud as a class
3. To give students practice reading orally
4. To evaluate students' oral reading
5. To preview the study questions for pp 21-40
6. To do the pre-reading vocabulary work for pp 21-40

Activity #1
You might begin by discussing the idea of a wasteland as a barren, desolate, and forlorn piece of country. Then try to get the students to extend their idea of a wasteland to life. What kind of life would resemble a physical wasteland? What kind of person would be living in a wasteland of the mind and soul? If one is living in a physical and/or spiritual wasteland, is it possible for that person to find a way out, to grow internally? If students grasp the idea of the wasteland theme, they will be better able to consider Stanley's life and predicament.

Activity #2
Have students read pp 3-20 out loud in class. You probably know the best way to choose readers from your class: pick students at random, ask for volunteers, or use whatever other method works best for your group. If you have not yet completed an oral reading evaluation for your students this marking period, this would be a good opportunity to do so. A form is included with this unit for your convenience. It probably is a good idea to share with students ahead of time the ways in which you are evaluating their reading skills. Try to make time to share your evaluations with students.

There should be enough time to complete all of the reading. However, if students do not complete reading through pp 3-20 in class, they should do so prior to your next class meeting.

Activity #3
Begin previewing the study questions and doing the pre-reading vocabulary work for pp 21-40. If you run out of time for the study questions and vocabulary work, tell students that they should have completed these tasks prior to the next class meeting.

Activity #4
Spend just a minute or two calling students' attention to the bulletin board materials that stress Stanley's continuing sense of aloneness, alienation, and desolation.

Lesson Four

Objectives
1. To recap the study questions and vocabulary from the last class
2. To review the main events and ideas from pp 3-20
3. To read pp 21-40 in class
4. To do an in-class activity defining what makes a good counselor

Activity #1
Spend just enough time on the study questions and vocabulary to assure that students are understanding the assignment and to prepare them for the reading in class.

Activity #2
Briefly review the main events and ideas from pp 3-20. Continue to examine the ideas of the wasteland and aloneness. In addition to any vocabulary words, you might ask students to pick out words in the text that stress the ideas of the wasteland and aloneness.

Activity #3
Have students read pp 21-40 of **Holes** out loud in class. Use the method of selecting student readers that works best for you. Continue the oral reading evaluations. Continue to share your evaluations with students, especially if students need a lot of improvement or if they demonstrate dramatic improvement.

Activity #4
Spend a little time with students talking about what makes a good counselor. What kind of person would students be likely to trust, listen to, and confide in? Ask students to write down at least three words each to describe a good counselor. Then spend a short time in class allowing students to explain and defend their word choices. If time permits, ask students if Mr. Pendanski seems to be a good counselor–based on pp 3-40. Do his personality and actions match their choices of words?

Lesson Five

Objectives
1. To review the main events and ideas from pp 21-40
2. To do study questions for pp 41-58
3. To do vocabulary work for pp 41-58
4. To assign the reading for pp 41-58

Activity #1
Briefly review the main events and ideas from pp 21-40. Try to be sure that students are following the author's back-and-forth movements from Stanley's present-day life at the camp to the lives of his ancestors. Ask if students have any questions about what is going on in the plot at this point.

Activity #2
Do the preview work for pp 41-58: study questions and vocabulary.

Activity #3
Assign pp 41-58 to be read at home.

Lesson Six

Objective
> To give students the opportunity to write to inform/explain

Activity #1
Have students complete Writing Assignment #1 (Writing to Inform/Explain). The directions for the assignment follow.

(Note for the teacher: Depending on which grade level you are teaching, this assignment, with its wasteland point of view, might be difficult for some students to grasp. Thus, the assignment has been clearly broken into three parts which should direct the student's understanding as well as make for easy organization. Also, while it is obvious that having the students read each other's rough drafts will perhaps help students to increase their own store of examples, it should also further increase all students' understanding of what is going on in the book so far.

Try to get the students' compositions back to them as soon as you can so that they can receive pointers on their writing. They will be writing another composition–this time at home–for Lesson Ten.

Witing Assignment #1 - Holes
(Writing to Inform/Explain)

PROMPT
In just twenty pages of **Holes**, Louis Sachar has made it clear that Stanley Yelnats is existing in a wasteland. So far, we might examine this wasteland in terms of the physical environment of Camp Green Lake, the people at the camp, and Stanley's life situation/culture (everything that made up his life prior to his going to the camp).

Your assignment is to write a composition to explain to the reader that Stanley is, in fact, existing in a wasteland. Although you should talk about each of the aspects of the wasteland (physical environment, people at the camp, and Stanley's life situation), you may introduce them in any order. Just be sure to give examples supporting each aspect and showing that Stanley is existing in a wasteland. It might help to pretend that your reader has not read the first twenty pages. Your job is to demonstrate to the reader that Stanley's world–in pp 3-20--is a wasteland.

PREWRITING
Begin by quickly re-reading the first twenty pages of the book. Make some notes as you re-read. Think about what it would be like to **be** Stanley, about how he feels about his parents, his home life, the events that have taken him to the camp, and about the people he encounters at the camp. And think about the camp itself (what it looks and feels like).

DRAFTING
Write an introductory paragraph designed to catch the reader's attention and to state your composition's main point: that Stanley Yelnats is existing in a wasteland. Write at least one paragraph discussing each aspect of the wasteland: one for physical environment, one for people at camp, and one for Stanley's life situation. Make sure that you give sufficient examples and that you are not simply quoting from the book. Write a concluding summary paragraph.

PROMPT
When you finish the rough draft of your paper, ask a student who sits near you to read it and to see if your main point is clearly expressed and supported by good examples. Then the student should tell you what he or she liked best about your work, which parts were difficult to understand, and ways in which your work could be improved. Re-read your paper considering your critic's comments and make the corrections you think are necessary.

PROOFREADING
Do a final proofreading of your paper, double-checking your grammar, spelling, organization, and the clarity of your ideas.

Writing Evaluation Form - Holes

Name _____ Date _____

Writing Assignment _____ Grade _____

Circle One for each item:

Topic interest	excellent	good	fair	poor
Overall organization	excellent	good	fair	poor
Clarity of expression	excellent	good	fair	poor
Grammar	excellent	good	fair	poor
Spelling	excellent	good	fair	poor
Punctuation	excellent	good	fair	poor

Strengths

Weaknesses

Comments/Suggestions

Lesson Seven

Objectives
1. To review pp 41-58
2. To have students write one paragraph about a single main point in pp 41-58
3. To do the preview work for pp 59-79: study questions and vocabulary

Activity #1
Review with students the main events of pp 41-58.

Activity #2
Have the students write one paragraph about a main point in pp 41-58, which they now have read and reviewed. The objects of writing the paragraph are to keep the students writing and to further clarify their understanding of the pages they have read. Some points that they might consider–if they don't easily come up with points themselves–are Stanley's being given a nickname, his letter to his mother, his fantasizing about the bully Derrick Dunne, the fossil Stanley finds, Mr. Pendanski's style of counseling, and the danger of the lizards at the camp.

Activity #3
This time you might have the students work in small groups to do the preview work for pp 59-79. If time permits, you might want to circulate among the groups to be sure that most of the students are participating.

Lesson Eight

Objectives
1. To read pp 59-79 in class
2. Discuss in class what Stanley learns about holes in terms of his overall growth
3. Do the preview work for pp 80-100: study questions and vocabulary
4. Assign pp 80-100 to be read at home

Activity #1
In order to vary the class readings, you might try going student by student, having each read one sentence from **Holes**. Thus, a student would read, "All too soon Stanley was back out on the lake, sticking his shovel into the dirt." Then the second student would read, "X-Ray was right: the third hole was the hardest." The next student would read, "So was the fourth hole." And so on until the class collectively has read pp 59-79. If you choose this method of reading out loud, you might also encourage the students to read with real feeling: thus, "And the sixth, and the..." would be read with a kind of despairing drudgery.

If you prefer simply to have students read out loud as you have done in earlier activities, that's fine too. Do what seems best for your students. Sometimes some variety will help to keep students' attention focused better.

Activity #2
Try to get students to see what Stanley learns about holes in terms of his overall growth. Throughout pp 59-79, Stanley begins to have revelations about what is going on around him. He starts to reason things out, to make a little sense of what is happening. He gives the gold tube to X-Ray, encourages X-Ray to use the find to get a whole day off from digging, finds out that the Warden is a woman who knows a lot about all the boys, sees how much authority the Warden has, questions the other boys' view of how the Warden spies on them, learns a little about Zero's background, etc. Perhaps his biggest revelation is the reason the boys are made to dig holes: "One thing was certain: They weren't just digging to 'build character.' They were definitely looking for something." Have a discussion with students focusing on what Stanley is learning at Camp Green Lake.

Activity #3
If time permits, do the preview work for pp 80-100 in class. If time is short, ask students to complete the preview work at home and to bring it to the next class.

Activity #4
Assign pp 80-100 to be read at home. From time to time, you might encourage students to read out loud at home, either for themselves or to a friend, a sibling, a parent, or whomever. As you know, some students learn best when they simply read and think about the written word whereas others learn best when they hear the words read out loud.

Lesson Nine

Objectives
1. To make sure that students are keeping up
2. To review pp 80-100
3. To discuss with students complexity of character development
4. To prepare students for the nonfiction reading assignment

Activity #1
See if students have questions about the preview work they are doing in and out of class. Take a few minutes for responses if necessary. Try to be sure that all students are understanding the book. This is a good time to note any students who aren't doing their work on a regular basis and to try to get them on track.

You may be collecting these preview exercises: if so, be sure that they are returned to students promptly for study purposes.

Activity #2
Review pp 80-100 that students have read at home.

Activity #3
Discuss, through the information that comes out from the beginning of the book through page 100, the complexity of Zero's character development.

Activity #4
Spend some time discussing the purposes and topics of the nonfiction reading assignment. Some purposes for doing the nonfiction reading are to enhance the students' knowledge, to supplement what they are learning through reading **Holes**, to encourage them to read on their own, and to make the book even more relevant to real life.

Topics to Choose for Nonfiction Reading Assignment - Holes

You may choose any of the following topics for your Nonfiction Reading Assignment. All of the topics are based in some way on **Holes**. If you wish to read about some other topics, you must clear it with your teacher *before you begin the assignment*.

1. Juvenile detention facilities
   (what they were like in the past, how they are in more modern times, what their purpose is, whether or not they serve a purpose, what they are like in other countries, etc.)

2. Learning to read
   (how many people in this country can read and write, how the US reading/writing rate compares to that in other countries, how reading and writing are taught in school, how students' reading and writing abilities are evaluated, the pleasures and/or agonies of reading during leisure time, etc.)

3. Counseling
   (how counselors relate to students, what makes a good counselor, what students want in a counselor, how counseling programs fit into school curriculums, etc.)

4. Reptiles and insects
   (reptiles and/or insects found in desert surroundings, the relative danger of reptiles and insects (lizards, spiders, scorpions, etc.), "good" reptiles and insects, etc.

5. The desert
   (deserts in this country and/or in other countries, how to survive in the desert, desert areas where modern development has taken place, etc.)

6. Girl Scouts
   (Girl Scout camps of the past and/or present, the Girl Scout movement in the US, how scouting has changed for girls, etc.)

7. Curses
   (do people really believe in curses, is it possible for put a curse on someone, curses of the past, etc.)

8. Gypsies
   (can Gypsies really foretell the future, what Gypsies exist in this country today, what Gypsy life is like, etc.)

Nonfiction Reading Topics - **Holes** - page 2

9. Parent/Child relationships
   (parent/child relationships at various ages, relationships between parents and children in other cultures, etc.)

10. Lullabies and nursery rhymes
    (lullabies and/or nursery rhymes of the past, do children today learn lullabies and nursery rhymes, if not what do they learn instead, etc.)

Lesson Ten

Objectives
1. To give students further time to discuss and begin research on the Nonfiction Reading Assignment
2. To give students the opportunity to write–at home this time–to express a personal opinion
3. To do the preview work in class for pp 101-123: short answer and vocabulary
4. To assign pp 101-123 to be read at home

Activity #1
If time allows, have students announce to the class what they intend to do for their Nonfiction Reading Assignment. Also, if students wish to write on topics not on the list (or even topics on the list that you feel will be inappropriate for specific students), this might be a good time to have students discuss their choices individually with you. Give students time to do some further reading for the assignment.

Activity #2
Make the personal opinion writing assignment. This should be a relatively easy assignment since it involves only an understanding of what students have read and their personal thoughts about themselves and how they want to be seen and understood. The directions for the assignment follow.

Activity #3
Do the preview work in class for pp 101-123.

Activity #4
Assign pp 101-123 to be read at home.

Writing Assignment #2
(Writing to Express a Personal Opinion)

PROMPT
In the reading you have done so far in **Holes**, you have come upon many nicknames and people's attitudes toward them: "Barf Bag," "Kissin'Kate Barlow," "Caveman," "Mom," "Zero," "X-Ray," "Magnet," "the Warden," and "Trout"–to name some. It seems that nearly everyone has a nickname at some time in his or her life. Some of the nicknames are positive and some are not. Some serve well at a particular time but would be inappropriate at another. Some make the people called by nicknames feel good about themselves; some make the people feel bad. Some nicknames are simply shortened real names or variants of real names: some examples are Bill or Willy for William, Betty or Liz for Elizabeth, Bob or Rob for Robert, Katie for Kathleen, Tommy for Thomas, Dick for Richard.

The question is, what would you like your nickname to be and why? Or, if you already have a nickname, how do you feel about it? If you have a nickname and don't like it, explain why you don't like it and tell what nickname you would like to have. If you have a nickname and like it a lot, explain why. If you don't want to share a current nickname in this piece of writing, just go back to the question of what you would like your nickname to be.

PREWRITING
Decide how you want to approach this assignment. Choose one option. Once you have chosen your point of view, figure out ways to explain it. Whichever option you pick, you should have lots of specific reasons why you feel the way you do.

DRAFTING
Write an introductory paragraph introducing the idea of nicknames in general and ending with a specific statement about the writing option you have chosen. Try to state your opinion and give three reasons to back it up. Then write at least one paragraph explaining and supporting each of your reasons. It is always good to give specific examples. Also, it is sometimes useful to use humor if you possibly can. And, finally, write a concluding paragraph in which you summarize what you have said in your essay.

PROMPT
When you finish the draft of your paper, ask someone to read it and see if your main point is clearly and convincingly expressed and supported by good examples. Your reader may be a friend, classmate, family member, or anyone else who might be a good reviewer. After reading your rough draft, he or she should tell you what he or she liked best about your work, which parts were difficult to understand, and ways in which your work could be improved. Reread your paper considering your critic's comments and make the corrections you think are necessary.

PROOFREADING
Do a final proofreading of your paper, double-checking your grammar, spelling, and organization.

Lesson Eleven

Objectives
1. To discuss briefly pp 101-123 (the end of PART ONE)
2. To set parameters for the Project
3. To do the preview work for pp 127-144

Activity #1
Discuss briefly pp 101-123, which mark the end of PART ONE. Try to be sure that students notice the unraveling of the plot concerning the real names and identities of Zero (Hector Zeroni) and Linda Miller (Linda Walker) and the information about Katherine Barlow's famous peaches and Sam's magically curative onions.

Activity #2
Introduce Project Juvenile Detention Centers to your students (details on the next page). Remember that this is an optional project. If you choose not to include it in your planning, you might instead assign the students to do one of the following: write a "real" letter from Stanley to his parents telling the truth about what is happening at Camp Green Lake; write a newspaper article, including headline, that exposes what is happening at the camp; pick their favorite (or least favorite) character in the book so far and write a composition that describes that character and explains why they chose him or her.

Activity #3
Do the preview work for pp 127-144: short answer and vocabulary.

Project Juvenile Detention Centers

Objectives

Project Juvenile Detention Centers is a total class project for use in conjunction with the book **Holes** by Louis Sachar. Since one of the main ideas in the book deals with the problems faced by a group of boys as they try to cope in a juvenile detention camp, this is a good opportunity to acquaint students with the resources and facilities for juvenile delinquents in your state. Today we hear about juvenile crime on television and in newspapers a lot. Murder is no longer a crime committed only by mature adults; very young children have been accused of killing people. But this project is concerned with so-called lesser crimes, such as incorrigibility, theft, vandalism, etc. The project is a way to make your students aware of the fact that more and more young people are being detained because of their crimes, to learn more about the needs of these young people, and to research what their state offers in the way of juvenile detention centers.

Students may use books to find useful information, or they may use the Internet if they have easy access to computers. If possible, students may even choose to interview police authorities in your town to find out firsthand how your area treats juvenile offenders.

A suggestion: Try to monitor the way in which your students respond to information they acquire. Some of the information they encounter may discuss very serious juvenile crime and very serious outcomes. If you think it prudent, you may even want to send a brief letter home to the students' families to let them know that your class is engaging in this project.

THE PROJECT

This project is separate from the rest of the unit on **Holes**, so you can either use it while you are reading and reviewing the book or as a separate mini-unit after you have completed the unit tests for **Holes**. Also, having it as a separate project enables you to either eliminate it or to use it, without disturbing the flow of the unit as a whole. If you choose not to use it, you may want to substitute a less complicated alternative project, a few of which are suggested under Activity #2 for Lesson Nine.

Assignment #1

Your local television station or newspaper should have some reports/articles on juvenile delinquency, youthful offenders, and juvenile detention centers in yours and other states. News magazines often contain articles as well. And, of course, you yourself might use the Internet if computer availability is not a problem. At any rate, find several reports/articles on juvenile crime and show them to your students. Try to present the situation of juvenile crime as clearly and truthfully as possible. Use the reports and articles as a springboard for a discussion of juvenile crime and the problems it poses to society.

Project Juvenile Detention - **Holes** - page 2

Assignment #2
As a class, write a letter to your police authorities inviting a representative to come to your class to discuss juvenile crime from their point of view. Even if juvenile crime is not a huge problem in your community, you can be sure that authorities have plans of action in place given all of the serious crimes that have taken place across the country in the last few years. Send the letter and then make any necessary follow-up phone calls to make arrangements for the visit.

Activity #3
After students have the information you gather on juvenile crime, send them to the library to do some research. If extensive information is not available in your school library, students may need to visit a community library. They might also find information in recently published encyclopedias and various magazines. However they secure the materials, each student should be able to read and summarize at least two articles on the topic. Hint: They might want to research the average age of juvenile offenders; whether or not gender plays a role in juvenile crime; what kind of facilities are available; what those facilities offer in terms of medical, mental, and educational services and how they foster social, emotional, intellectual, and physical development; and how the facilities deal with security, safety, supervision, training of staff, and physical accommodations; whether or not stays in juvenile detention centers contribute to the rehabilitation of juvenile offenders or not, etc.

Assignment #4
After students have done their research, have them give brief oral reports about the articles they have read so that all students are exposed to the wealth of information that has been collectively read.

Assignment #5
Host the person who was invited to class in Assignment #2. This assignment should be done prior to undertaking Assignment #6.

Assignment #6
Divide students into groups of five or six. Explain that their job is to make a list of at least three important aspects of detaining juvenile offenders and to brainstorm ways that those aspects might be addressed.

Students might focus, for example, on how to make a facility secure without making it be just like a prison; how to get the juveniles to interact with each other in ways that will help them to adjust better when they are released; how to offer counseling that will help offenders to adjust emotionally; etc.

Appropriate class time will need to be spent on this brainstorming.

Project Juvenile Detention - **Holes** - page 3

After the brainstorming has been done, have each student focus on one aspect that seems to him or her to be most important. Then students should suggest ways in which they might address that aspect in a productive way: letter writing, personally volunteering, writing a newspaper article, having speakers talk at local schools, other educational campaigns, etc. Although the students need not actually send the letters or articles, personally volunteer, engage speakers, or mount other educational campaigns, they should be able to suggest clearly how such things would be done.

Assignment #7
After the project is finished, have a short wrap-up to allow students to discuss the value of the project overall. Try to get students to articulate what they learned from participating in the project. Have the students write a few sentences explaining what the project meant to them.
(All written materials generated by the project should be turned in to you on a date that you specify.)

Lesson Twelve

Objectives
1. To read pp 127-144 in class and to evaluate student reading
2. To review the main ideas, events, and characterizations in pp 3-144 of **Holes**
3. To have students exercise their critical thinking skills.

Activity #1
Choose students to read out loud pp 127-144. Use the evaluation forms if you choose to do so.

Activity #2
Review with students the main ideas, events, and characterizations in pp 3-144 of **Holes**.

(The first two objectives in Lesson Twelve should be achieved easily and rather quickly. This is a good time to be sure that all students are keeping up with the story line, main ideas, and characterizations in the book.)

Activity #3
Choose some questions from the Extra Discussion Questions/Writing Assignments which seem most appropriate for your students. A class discussion of these questions is most effective if students have been given the opportunity to formulate answers to the questions prior to the discussion. To this end, you may either have all the students formulate answers to all the questions you choose, divide your class into groups and assign one or more questions to each group, or you could assign one question to each student in your class. The option you choose will make a difference in the amount of class time needed for this activity.

After students have had ample time to formulate answers to the questions, begin your class discussion of the questions and the ideas presented by them. Be sure students take notes during the discussion so they have information to study for the unit test.

Extra Discussion Questions/Writing Assignments - Holes

Interpretive

1. From whose point of view is **Holes** told? How might the story be different if Stanley himself were narrating it? What if it were told from Zero's point of view? The Warden's?

2. How is irony used in **Holes**? The first ironic information we are given is that Camp Green Lake is not a camp, is not green, and does not have a lake. What effect is achieved by calling the place Camp Green Lake? What other irony is introduced in the novel?

3. Try to analyze the character of Stanley Yelnats. What is he like at the beginning of the story? How does his character change as the story progresses? What details about Stanley does Sachar give the reader?

4. What are the main conflicts in the novel and how are they resolved?

5. The end of the novel is filled with suspense. How does Sachar build suspense?

6. Is the outcome of the book surprising? Is it easy or hard to figure out ahead of time how the book will end?

Critical

7. Why did Sachar call the book **Holes**? Is the novel really about holes? What kind of holes might Sachar be thinking of besides the physical holes the boys are forced to dig?

8. Stanley is described as a victim from the beginning of the book. How does his victimization color the reader's view of him?

9. Compare and contrast Mr. Pendanski and Mr. Sir. Are they more often alike or different?

10. Think about Sachar's writing style. How does the simplicity of his writing contribute to the reader's enjoyment and understanding of the novel?

11. What is the most important theme in the novel? Some possibilities are aloneness, courage, growth, maturity, friendship, desperation, and loyalty.

12. How would Stanley's life have been different had he not gone out after Zero?

Extra Discussion - **Holes** - page 2

Critical/Personal Response

13. Do you think that the action in **Holes** could actually take place today?

14. If you were Stanley, would you have decided to help Zero?

15. Which character in the novel did you find most believable? Tell why.

Personal Response

16. With which character in **Holes** do you most identify? Tell why.

17. Which character in **Holes** is the kindest? the strongest? the weakest? the most admirable? the most likeable? Explain your choice.

18. What would you do if you were placed in Stanley's position? Explain in detail.

19. Which character in the book would you choose as a friend? Tell why.

20. Is **Holes** a good novel, in your opinion? Explain why or why not.

Extra Discussion - **Holes** - page 3

Quotations and Interesting Parts of the Novel

21. Stanley Yelnats was given a choice. The judge said, "You may go to jail, or you may go to Camp Green Lake."
 Stanley was from a poor family. He had never been to camp before.

22. But perhaps that was part of the curse as well. If Stanley and his father weren't always so hopeful, then it wouldn't hurt so much every time their hopes were crushed.

23. "You thirsty?" asked Mr. Sir.
 "Yes, Mr. Sir," Stanley said gratefully.
 "Well, you better get used to it. You're going to be thirsty for the next eighteen months."

24. "I see you're looking at my gun. Don't worry. I'm not going to shoot you." He tapped his holster. "This is for yellow-spotted lizards. I wouldn't waste a bullet on you."

25. "You're not looking for anything. You're digging to build character. It's just if you find anything, the Warden would like to know about it."

26. "Vacancies don't last long at Camp Green Lake."

27. "You're all special in your own way," he said. "You've all got something to offer...Even you Zero. You're not completely worthless."

28. Kate Barlow died laughing.

29. He heard the sound of approaching cars.
 Mr. Sir and the Warden heard it as well.
 "You think it's them?" asked the Warden.
 "It ain't Girl Scouts selling cookies," said Mr. Sir.

Lesson Thirteen

Objectives
1. To assign the preview work for pp 145-159 to be done at home
2. To assign pp 145-159 to be read at home
3. To do a role-playing exercise

Activity #1
Assign the preview work for pp 145-159: short answer and vocabulary

Activity #2
Assign pp 145-159.

Activity #3
The role-playing exercise is designed to help the students to understand the characters in **Holes** better by envisioning them in different contexts. Except for making the assignments in Activities #1 and #2, try to put aside one entire class to achieve Objective 3. What you are going to do is ask some of your students to do some role playing in front of the rest of the class. Because not everyone will have the opportunity to play a role in class, the other students will learn from observing. Both actors and observers should be encouraged to think about how the characters are going to act in each scenario. You will be the best judge of which students can be relied on to carry out the assignment with a reasonable degree of understanding and comfort.

Don't worry that you don't have enough time to accommodate this kind of role playing. Its object is not to rehearse or spend a lot of time preparing for the role playing. It is, instead, to think through very quickly how a character will act based on which students already know about him or her.

This activity will work best if you try to prepare the students to have a good time doing it. Make sure they realize that there is no totally right or totally wrong way to do the activity. Instead, they should listen closely to the scenarios that you lay out, think very quickly about how each assigned character would react to each, and then pretend to *be* that character to the best of their ability.

Choose the scenarios that you think your students will best understand. You may do only one of the scenarios or all three. If you want, you can even makeup new scenarios, with or without your students' help. Again, there is no right or wrong here. You are just moving the characters around a little bit in order to let students look at them a little differently and understand them a little bit better.

Read the scenario. Give students three to five minutes to prepare, and then give them five minutes to act out the scenario. The ONLY requirement is that students try as hard as possible to keep the character as he or she behaved in the pages assigned so far in **Holes**.

Lesson Thirteen - **Holes** - page 2

Scenario #1 The Warden and Stanley
The Warden has invited Stanley to come to her room. She proposes that she will have him released back into the custody of his parents if he will spy on the other boys and report back to her on their conversations and actions for the next month. Stanley doesn't want to take part in deception against the other boys, but he is extremely anxious to get out of Camp Green Lake. ***Have the Warden make her proposal and have Stanley respond. Have counter-responses for as long as time allows.***

Scenario #2 Stanley and his mother
The Warden has decided that it would be good for camp image to allow each boy to make a phone call to his parents. Naturally, because she knows she now has the boys totally under her control and in fear of her, she expects them to say what will make Camp Green Lake sound like a real camp. She tells the boys that she will be listening in on their calls and will punish boys who do not paint a good picture of their time at Camp Green Lake. ***Have Stanley phone his mother and have the two of them discuss Camp Green Lake and Stanley's stay there.***

Scenario #3 Katherine Barlow and the sheriff
The sheriff tells Katherine Barlow that he will allow Sam to leave Green Lake peacefully if she will agree to lecture her all-white students on the evils of black people. Obviously Katherine doesn't want to do what the sheriff wants, nor does she believe that black people are evil, but she does understand that the sheriff's suggestion is a way of saving both herself and Sam. ***Have the sheriff make his suggestion and have Katherine respond. Have counter-responses for as long as time allows.***

Lesson Fourteen

Objectives
1. To review pp 145-159
2. To do the preview work for pp 160-181
3. To read pp 160-181 in class.
4. To have students give oral reports on the nonfiction reading assignment

Activity #1
Briefly review pp 145-159.

Activity #2
Do the preview work for pp 160-181 as a class: short answer and vocabulary

Activity #3
Read pp 160-181 in class.

Activity #4
Allow students to give brief oral reports on their nonfiction reading.

Lesson Fifteen

Objectives
1. To continue oral reports on nonfiction reading assignment
2. To review pp 160-181

Activity #1
Allow students to continue to give brief oral reports on their nonfiction reading.

Activity #2
Review the main events, ideas, and characterizations in pp 160-181.

Lesson Sixteen

Objective
1. To do the preview work on pp 182-197
2. To catch up on loose ends

Activity #1
Do the preview work on pp 182-197: short answer and vocabulary

Activity #2
Catch up on any loose ends. Think about whether or not you need to give a quiz, answer students' questions, follow up on any leftover odds and ends from previous lessons, etc.

Lesson Seventeen

Objectives
1. To read pp 182-197
2. To do the preview work on pp 198-225
3. To assign pp 198-225 to be read at home
4. To give students the opportunity to report on their projects

Activity #1
Have students read pp 182-197 out loud.

Activity #2

Do the preview work on pp 198-225 as a class: short answer and vocabulary.

Activity #4
Assign pp 198-225 to be read at home. Remind students of the benefits of their reading out loud to someone at home.

Activity #5
Have students report on their projects. Because of time restraints, students should be encouraged to be brief–a few minutes per students will have to suffice.

Lesson Eighteen

Objectives
1. To continue to give students the opportunity to report on their projects
2. To make sure that students have understood the book, **Holes**

Activity #1
Have students continue to report briefly on their projects.

Activity #2
Ask a few questions to be sure that students have understood the main events, ideas, and characterizations of the book.

Lesson Nineteen

Objective
1. To continue to give students the opportunity to report on their projects
2. To do a vocabulary review for the whole book

Activity #1
Continue with the reports on the class project.

Activity #2
Because the vocabulary in **Holes** is not, overall, highly challenging, your students may or may not need a lengthy review before the unit tests. However you choose to review, you may want to pick one or more of the vocabulary review activities listed on the next page and spend the rest of the class period as directed in the activity. Some additional materials for these review activities are located in the Vocabulary Resource Materials at the end of this unit.

Vocabulary Review Activities

1. Divide your class into two teams and have an old-fashioned spelling or definition bee.

2. Give each of your students (or students in groups of two, three, or four) a Vocabulary Word Search Puzzle based on **Holes**. The person or group to find all of the vocabulary words in the puzzle first wins.

3. Give students a **Holes** Vocabulary Word Search Puzzle without the word list. The person or group to find the most vocabulary words in the puzzle wins.

4. Use a **Holes** Vocabulary Crossword Puzzle. Put a puzzle onto a transparency on the overhead projector so everyone can see it and do the puzzle together as a class.

5. Give students a **Holes** Vocabulary Matching Worksheet to do.

6. Divide your class into two teams. Use **Holes** vocabulary words with their letters jumbled as a word list. Student 1 from Team A faces off against Student 1 from Team B. You write the first jumbled word on the board. The first student (1A or 1B) to unscramble the word wins the chance for his or her team to score points. If 1A wins the jumble, go to 2A and give him or her a definition. He or she must give you the correct spelling of the vocabulary word which fits that definition. If he or she does, Team A scores a point, and you give 3A a definition for which you expect a correctly spelled matching vocabulary word. Continue giving Team A definitions until some team member makes an incorrect response. An incorrect response sends the game back to the jumbled-word face-off, this time with students 2A and 2B. Instead of repeating giving definitions to the first few students of each team, continue with the student after the one who gave the last incorrect response on the team. For example, if Team B wins the jumbled-word face-off and student 5B gave the last incorrect answer for Team B, you would start this round of definition questions with student 6B and so on. The team with the most points wins!

7. Have students write a story in which they correctly use as many vocabulary words as possible. Have students read their compositions orally. Post the most original compositions on your bulletin board.

Lesson Twenty

Objective
> To give students the opportunity to write to persuade

Activity #1

Have students complete Writing Assignment #3 (Writing to Persuade). You may use the directions that follow in this unit.

Writing Assignment #3 - Holes
(Writing to Persuade)

PROMPT
Now that you have finished reading and discussing **Holes** in its entirety, you have no doubt formed some opinions about it. What you are going to do now is to write to persuade. In order to do that, you need to choose an argument to make. Pick one of the following topics. You will be arguing strongly pro or con that:

1. Stanley Yelnats is a very believable (or unbelievable) character.
2. The ending of the book is very believable (or unbelievable).
3. The book is filled with too many coincidences.
4. The many coincidences in **Holes** made the book fun to read.
5. **Holes** is (or is not) suitable for a reader at my age level.
6. **Holes** is a book about personal success (or personal failure).

PREWRITING
Choose your topic and decide how you want to argue your issue. Make sure that you choose a point of view that you believe in. By brainstorming, make a list of all of the reasons you believe as you do. Then try to combine any of the reasons into groups of reasons. Then choose your three strongest points.

DRAFTING
Write an introductory paragraph in which you state as firmly as possible your argument. After reading your introductory paragraph, a reader should know exactly where you stand on the issue being discussed. Then write one paragraph explaining each of your reasons. Make sure that you have explained your reasons thoroughly enough that you don't leave lots of questions in the mind of the read. Write as forcefully as possible throughout. And finally, write a concluding paragraph in which you summarize your main points and conclude your argument.

PROMPT
When you finish the rough draft of your paper, ask a student who sits near you to read it. You want to know if you have argued your point well, not whether the other student necessarily agrees with your point. After reading your rough draft, he or she should tell you what he or she liked best about your work, which parts were difficult to understand, and ways in which your work could be improved. Reread your paper considering your critic's comments and make the corrections you think are necessary.

PROOFREADING
Do a final proofreading of your paper, double-checking your grammar, spelling, organization, and the clarity of your ideas.

UNIT TESTS

Short Answer Unit Test #1 - Holes

I. Matching/Identify

___ "Mom" A. Stanley's great-great-grandfather

___ Elya B. Stanley's family

___ Yelnats C. One-legged gypsy

___ Katherine Barlow D. Sam's donkey

___ "Sweet Feet" E. Stanley's counselor

___ The original Mary Lou F. School teacher turned robber

___ Katherine Barlow G. Clyde Livingston's nickname

___ Madame Zeroni H. Mr. Pendanski's nickname

II. Short Answer

1. Who supposedly is to blame for Stanley's bad luck in being convicted of a crime?

2. What is especially unusual about Stanley Yelnats' name?

3. What did Mr. Pendanski say was the reason the boys were digging holes?

4. Why was Stanley glad that the other boys called him "Caveman"?

5. What was Stanley's big revelation about Zero?

6. What did the Warden say was the special ingredient in her red nail polish?

Short Answer Unit Test #1 - **Holes** - page 2

7. What special remedy did Sam offer to the people of Green Lake?

8. What did Stanley think he saw in the rock formation on the mountain peak?

9. What did Zero and Stanley eat to stay alive?

10. What will become of Camp Green Lake?

III. Essay
What does Stanley learn at Camp Green Lake about personal courage and accountability? Explain in detail using examples from the novel.

Short Answer Unit Test #1 - **Holes** - page 3

IV. Vocabulary

Listen to the vocabulary words and spell them. After you have spelled all the words, go back and write down the definitions.

1.

2.

3.

4.

5.

6.

7.

8.

9.

10.

Key - Short Answer Unit Test #1 - Holes

I. Matching/Identify

_H_	"Mom"	A.	Stanley's great-great-grandfather
_A_	Elya	B.	Stanley's family
_B_	Yelnats	C.	One-legged gypsy
_E_	Katherine Barlow	D.	Sam's donkey
_G_	"Sweet Feet"	E.	Stanley's counselor
_D_	The original Mary Lou	F.	School teacher turned robber
_F_	Katherine Barlow	G.	Clyde Livingston's nickname
_C_	Madame Zeroni	H.	Mr. Pendanski's nickname

II. Short Answer

1. Who supposedly is to blame for Stanley's bad luck in being convicted of a crime?
   Stanley's no-good-dirty-rotten-pig-stealing-great-great-grandfather is to blame.

2. What is especially unusual about Stanley Yelnats' name?
   His name is spelled the same frontward and backward.

3. What did Mr. Pendanski say was the reason the boys were digging holes?
   He said they were digging holes to build character.

4. Why was Stanley glad that the other boys called him "Caveman"?
   He was glad because the nickname meant that the boys had accepted him.

5. What was Stanley's big revelation about Zero?
   Stanley learned that Zero couldn't read.

6. What did the Warden say was the special ingredient in her red nail polish?
   She said it was rattlesnake venom.

7. What special remedy did Sam offer to the people of Green Lake?
   He offered them onions and products made of onions.

Key - Short Answer Unit Test #1 - **Holes** - page 2

8. What did Stanley think he saw in the rock formation on the mountain peak?
   He thought he saw a giant fist, with the thumb sticking straight up.

9. What did Zero and Stanley eat to stay alive?
   They ate onions from the meadow.

10. What will become of Camp Green Lake?
    In a few years it will become a Girl Scout camp.

III. Essay
   What does Stanley learn at Camp Green Lake about personal courage and accountability? Explain in detail using examples from the novel.

IV. Vocabulary
   Choose 10 vocabulary words to dictate to the students. Write them here if you wish.

Short Answer Unit Test #2 - Holes

I. Matching/Identify

_____ Yelnats   A. School teacher turned robber

_____ Madame Zeroni   B. Mr. Pendanski's nickname

_____ Mr. Pendanski   C. Stanley's family

_____ "Sweet Feet"   D. One-legged gypsy

_____ "Mom"   E. Stanley's great-great-grandfather

_____ Original Mary Lou   F. Stanley's counselor

_____ Elya   G. Clyde Livingston's nickname

_____ Katherine Barlow   H. Sam's the Onion Man's donkey

II. Short Answer

1. Who put a curse on the Yelnats family?

2. Who supposedly robbed the stagecoach of the first Stanley Yelnats?

3. What was Stanley's father trying to invent?

4. What was Mr. Sir's favorite expression?

5. What special prize did Miss Katherine Barlow win every Fourth of July?

6. What did Zero do in exchange for Stanley's teaching him to read and write?

7. What was the "sploosh" that Zero had been drinking?

Short Answer Unit Test #2 - **Holes** - page 2

8. How were Stanley and Zero finally rescued?

9. Approximately how much money did Stanley and Zero each receive?

10. What was the name of Stanley's father's invention to cure bad smelling feet?

III. Quotations: Identify the speaker and briefly explain the significance of the quotes.
Choices of speakers:

Hector Zeroni's mother	Sam the Onion Man	Katherine Barlow
Mr. Sir	Mr. Pendanski	Madame Zeroni
Zero	The Warden	The Sheriff

1. "I see you're looking at my gun. Don't worry. I'm not going to shoot you." He tapped his holster. "This is for yellow-spotted lizards. I wouldn't waste a bullet on you."

2. "They all have nicknames," explained _____. "However, I prefer to use the names their parents gave them–the names that *society will recognize them by* when they return to become useful and hardworking members of society."

3. "You're not looking for anything. You're digging to build character. It's just if you find anything, the Warden would like to know about it."

4. "I want you to carry me up the mountain. I want to drink from the stream, and I want you to sing the song to me."

5. "You're all special in your own way," he said. "You've all got something to offer. You have to think about what you want to do, then do it. Even you Zero. You're not completely worthless."

Short Answer Unit Test #2 - **Holes** - page 3

6. "If you must know," said _____, "I liked it better when you smoked."

7. "I can fix that."

8. "Well, then you'll have to hang me, too," said _____. "Because I kissed him back."

9. "I don't know what happened to my mother," _____ said. "She left and never came back."

10. "If only, if only, the moon speaks no reply;
    Reflecting the sun and all that's gone by.
    Be strong my weary wolf, turn around boldly.
    Fly high, my baby bird,
    My angel, my only."

Short Answer Unit Test #2 - **Holes** - page 4

IV. Vocabulary

　　Listen to the vocabulary words and spell them. After you have spelled all the words, go back and write down the definitions.

1.

2.

3.

4.

5.

6.

7.

8.

9.

10.

Key - Short Answer Unit Test #2 - Holes

I. Matching/Identify

__C__	Yelnats	A.	School teacher turned robber
__D__	Madame Zeroni	B.	Mr. Pendanski's nickname
__F__	Mr. Pendanski	C.	Stanley's family
__G__	"Sweet Feet"	D.	One-legged gypsy
__B__	"Mom"	E.	Stanley's great-great-grandfather
__H__	Original Mary Lou	F.	Stanley's counselor
__E__	Elya	G.	Clyde Livingston's nickname
__A__	Katherine Barlow	H.	Sam's the Onion Man's donkey

II. Short Answer

1. Who put a curse on the Yelnats family?
   A one-legged gypsy named Madame Zeroni put the curse on the family.

2. Who supposedly robbed the stagecoach of the first Stanley Yelnats?
   Kissin' Kate Barlow was said to have robbed his stagecoach.

3. What was Stanley's father trying to invent?
   He was trying to invent a way to recycle old sneakers.

4. What was Mr. Sir's favorite expression?
   He said that Camp Green Lake wasn't a Girl Scout camp.

5. What special prize did Miss Katherine Barlow win every Fourth of July?
   She won a prize for her spiced peaches.

6. What did Zero do in exchange for Stanley's teaching him to read and write?
   Zero dug some of Stanley's holes for him each day.

7. What was the "sploosh" that Zero had been drinking?
   It was hundred-year-old peach nectar.

Key - Short Answer Unit Test #2 - **Holes** - page 2

8. How were Stanley and Zero finally rescued?
   Stanley's lawyer and the Texas Attorney General showed up.

9. Approximately how much money did Stanley and Zero each receive?
   Stanley and Zero each received a little less than a million dollars.

10. What was the name of Stanley's father's invention to cure bad smelling feet?
    The product was called "Sploosh."

III. Quotations: Identify the speaker and briefly explain the significance of the quotes.
   Choices of speakers:

Hector Zeroni's mother	Sam the Onion Man	Katherine Barlow
Mr. Sir	Mr. Pendanski	Madame Zeroni
Zero	The Warden	The Sheriff

1. "I see you're looking at my gun. Don't worry. I'm not going to shoot you." He tapped his holster. "This is for yellow-spotted lizards. I wouldn't waste a bullet on you."
   Mr. Sir

2. "They all have nicknames," explained _____. "However, I prefer to use the names their parents gave them–the names that *society will recognize them by* when they return to become useful and hardworking members of society."
   Mr. Pendanski

3. "You're not looking for anything. You're digging to build character. It's just if you find anything, the Warden would like to know about it."
   Mr. Pendanski

4. "I want you to carry me up the mountain. I want to drink from the stream, and I want you to sing the song to me."
   Madame Zeroni

5. "You're all special in your own way," he said. "You've all got something to offer. You have to think about what you want to do, then do it. Even you Zero. You're not completely worthless."
   Mr. Pendanski

Key- Short Answer Unit Test #2 - **Holes** - page 3

6. "If you must know," said _____, "I liked it better when you smoked."
   The Warden

7. "I can fix that."
   Sam the Onion Man

8. "Well, then you'll have to hang me, too," said _____. "Because I kissed him back."
   Katherine Barlow

9. "I don't know what happened to my mother," _____ said. "She left and never came back."
   Zero

10. "If only, if only, the moon speaks no reply;
    Reflecting the sun and all that's gone by.
    Be strong my weary wolf, turn around boldly.
    Fly high, my baby bird,
    My angel, my only."

    Zero's mother

IV. Vocabulary
    Choose ten vocabulary words to dictate to your students. Write them here if you wish.

Advanced Short Answer Unit Test - Holes

I.   Matching/Identify

_____ Yelnats   A.   School teacher turned robber

_____ Madame Zeroni   B.   Mr. Pendanski's nickname

_____ Mr. Pendanski   C.   Stanley's family

_____ "Sweet Feet"   D.   One-legged gypsy

_____ "Mom"   E.   Stanley's great-great-grandfather

_____ Original Mary Lou   F.   Stanley's counselor

_____ Elya   G.   Clyde Livingston's nickname

_____ Katherine Barlow   H.   Sam's the Onion Man's donkey

II. Short Answer

1.   Why did Sachar call the book **Holes**? Is the novel really about holes? What kind of holes might Sachar be thinking of besides the physical holes the boys are forced to dig?

2.   Stanley is described as a victim from the beginning of the book. How does his victimization color the reader's view of him?

Advanced Short Answer Unit Test - **Holes** - page 2

3. Compare and contrast Mr. Pendanski and Mr. Sir? Are they more often alike or different?

4. Think about Sachar's writing style. How does the simplicity of his writing contribute to the reader's enjoyment and understanding of the novel?

5. What is the most important theme in the novel? Some possibilities are aloneness, courage, growth, maturity, friendship, desperation, and loyalty.

6. How would Stanley's life have been different had he not gone out after Zero?

Advanced Short Answer Unit Test - **Holes** - page 3

III. Quotations: Explain the importance and meaning of the following quotations.

1. Stanley Yelnats was given a choice. The judge said, "You may go to jail, or you may go to Camp Green Lake." Stanley was from a poor family...had never been to camp before.

2.. But perhaps that was part of the curse as well. If Stanley and his father weren't always so hopeful, then it wouldn't hurt so much every time their hopes were crushed.

3. "You thirsty?" asked Mr. Sir.
   "Yes, Mr. Sir," Stanley said gratefully.
   "Well, you better get used to it. You're going to be thirsty for the next eighteen months."

4. "I see you're looking at my gun. Don't worry. I'm not going to shoot you." He tapped his holster. "This is for yellow-spotted lizards. I wouldn't waste a bullet on you."

5. "You're not looking for anything. You're digging to build character. It's just if you find anything, the Warden would like to know about it."

6. "Vacancies don't last long at Camp Green Lake."

7. "You're all special in your own way," he said. "You've all got something to offer...Even you Zero. You're not completely worthless."

Advanced Short Answer Unit Test - **Holes** - page 4

IV.	Vocabulary
	Listen to the vocabulary words and write them down. After you have written down all of the words, write a paragraph in which you use all the words. The paragraph must in some way relate to **Holes**,

Key - Advanced Short Answer Test - Holes

Matching/Identify answers can be found in Key: Short Answer Unit Test #2

Short Answers are subjective.

Explanations of Quotations are also subjective.

Vocabulary definitions may be found in other keys; the students' paragraphs are subjective.

Unit Test - Holes
Multiple Choice - Matching #1

I. Matching

_____ 1. Yelnats   A. School teacher turned robber

_____ 2. Madame Zeroni   B. Mr. Pendanski's nickname

_____ 3. Mr. Pendanski   C. Stanley's family

_____ 4. "Sweet Feet"   D. One-legged gypsy

_____ 5. "Mom"   E. Stanley's great-great-grandfather

_____ 6. Original Mary Lou   F. Stanley's counselor

_____ 7. Elya   G. Clyde Livingston's nickname

_____ 8. Katherine Barlow   H. Sam's the Onion Man's donkey

II. Multiple Choice

1. Who supposedly is to blame for Stanley's bad luck in being convicted of a crime?
    a. His mother
    b. His father
    c. His great-grandfather's friend
    d. His no-good-dirty-rotten-pig-stealing-great-great-grandfather

2. What is especially unusual about Stanley Yelnats' name?
    a. It is spelled the same frontward and backward.
    b. It has the same number of letters in his first and last names.
    c. It is an alias for his real name, Igor Barkov.
    d. Mr. Sir's brother-in-law has the same name.

3. What did Mr. Pendanski say was the reason the boys were digging holes?
    a. To have a place to bury the lizards
    b. To build character
    c. To make the Warden smile
    d. To get an extra shower in the evening

Multiple Choice Unit Test #1 - **Holes** - page 2

4. Why was Stanley glad that the other boys called him "Caveman"?
    a. Because the name made him feel strong
    b. Because he felt like he lived in a cave
    c. Because the nickname meant that the boys had accepted him
    d. Because it was better than being called "Barf Bag"

5. What was Stanley's big revelation about Zero?
    a. He really was dumb.
    b. He couldn't read.
    c. He should have been sent home months ago.
    d. His mother had been looking for him for months.

6. What did the Warden say was the special ingredient in her red nail polish?
    a. Rattlesnake venom
    b. Varnish
    c. Red food coloring
    d. Lizard blood

7. What special remedy did Sam offer to the people of Green Lake?
    a. Cold compresses
    b. Onions and products made of onions
    c. Peach juice
    d. Special water

8. What did Stanley think he saw in the rock formation on the mountain peak?
    a. His mother's face
    b. A giant fist, with the thumb sticking straight up
    c. Zero's face
    d. His great-great-grandfather's pig

9. What did Zero and Stanley eat to stay alive?
    a. Fish from a stream
    b. Sunflower seeds
    c. Peaches
    d. Onions from the meadow

10. What will become of Camp Green Lake?
    a. It will be closed and bulldozed.
    b. It will be used as a place for rookie baseball players to train.
    c. It will be used as a minimum security prison for men.
    d. It will become a Girl Scout camp.

Multiple Choice Unit Test #1 - **Holes** - page 3

III. Essay - pick one of two choices:
  A. Discuss which character in **Holes** you believe Louis Sachar likes best and explain through specific details why you made this choice.

OR

  B. Discuss which character in **Holes** you believe would be most successful in getting ahead in today's world. Explain through specific details why you made this choice.

Multiple Choice Unit Test #1 - **Holes** - page 4

IV. Vocabulary (Matching)

1. wasteland
2. perseverance
3. humiliating
4. preposterous
5. sprawled
6. barren
7. dread
8. writhed
9. concoctions
10. loot
11. feeble
12. precarious
13. refuge
14. engraved
15. lopsided
16. mirage
17. protruding
18. comprehend
19. inexplicable
20. jurisdiction

A. spread out in straggling or disordered fashion
B. dangerously lacking in security or stability
C. area of authority or control
D. carved, cut, etched into something
E. not giving up
F. not able to be explained or interpreted
G. uncultivated or desolate country
H. sticking, jutting out
I. being disgraced
J. absurd, ridiculous
K. heavier, larger on one side than on the other
L. something illusory, deceptive
M. sterile, dull, unfruitful
N. twisted, squirmed
O. in terror of, anticipated with fear, alarm, reluctance
P. preparations made by mixing ingredients
Q. stolen goods
R. protection or shelter
S. lacking strength
T. understand

Unit Test - Holes
Multiple Choice - Matching #2

I. Matching

_____ 1. Elya   A. School teacher turned robber

_____ 2. Mr. Pendanski   B. Mr. Pendanski's nickname

_____ 3. Katherine Barlow   C. Stanley's family

_____ 4. Madame Zeroni   D. One-legged gypsy

_____ 5. "Mom"   E. Stanley's great-great-grandfather

_____ 6. "Sweet Feet"   F. Stanley's counselor

_____ 7. Original Mary Lou   G. Clyde Livingston's nickname

_____ 8. Yelnats   H. Sam's the Onion Man's donkey

II. Multiple Choice

1. Who put a curse on the Yelnats family?
   a. Mr. Pendanski
   b. The Warden
   c. A one-legged gypsy named Madame Zeroni
   d. His no-good-dirty-rotten-pig-stealing-great-great-grandfather

2. Who supposedly robbed the stagecoach of the first Stanley Yelnats?
   a. Mr. Pendanski's best friend
   b. Sam the Onion Man
   c. Kissin' Kate Barlow
   d. A one-legged gypsy

3. What was Stanley's father trying to invent?
   a. A new way to feed pigs
   b. A way to recycle old sneakers
   c. A way to transport pigs to market safely
   d. A way to recycle newspapers

Multiple Choice Test #2 - **Holes** - page 2

4. What was Mr. Sir's favorite expression?
    a. He said that the boys were losers.
    b. He said that Camp Green Lake wasn't a Girl Scout camp.
    c. He said that the boys were building character every day.
    d. He said that he hated the Warden.

5. What special prize did Miss Katherine Barlow win every Fourth of July?
    a. A special flag
    b. A huge onion
    c. A prize for her special peaches
    d. A prize for being the prettiest woman in town

6. What did Zero do in exchange for Stanley's teaching him to read and write?
    a. Zero recommended Stanley to all of the other boys who couldn't read and write.
    b. Zero said nice things about Stanley to the Warden.
    c. Zero dug some of Stanley's holes for him each day.
    d. Zero promised to write a note to Stanley's parents.

7. What was the "sploosh" that Zero had been drinking?
    a. Hundred-year-old onion juice
    b. Old dirty water
    c. Hundred-year-old peach nectar
    d. Carrot juice

8. How were Stanley and Zero finally rescued?
    a. Stanley's parents showed up.
    b. Zero's mother sent a telegram asking for information.
    c. Mr. Pendanski decided to help them escape.
    d. Stanley's lawyer and the Texas Attorney General showed up.

9. Approximately how much money did Stanley and Zero each receive?
    a. About fifty thousand dollars
    b. Nearly seventy-five thousand dollars
    c. Only about thirty thousand dollars
    d. A little less than a million dollars

10. What was the name of Stanley's father's invention to cure bad smelling feet?
    a. "Sweet Feet"
    b. "Peachy Smell"
    c. "Sploosh"
    d. "Zero's Revenge"

Multiple Choice Unit Test #2 - **Holes** - page 3

III. Quotations: Identify the speaker

Choices of speakers:
(A) Hector Zeroni's mother   (D) Sam the Onion Man   (G) Katherine Barlow
(B) Mr. Sir   (E) Mr. Pendanski   (H) Madame Zeroni
(C) Zero   (F) The Warden   (I) The Sheriff

1. "I see you're looking at my gun. Don't worry. I'm not going to shoot you." He tapped his holster. "This is for yellow-spotted lizards. I wouldn't waste a bullet on you."

2. "They all have nicknames," explained _____. "However, I prefer to use the names their parents gave them–the names that *society will recognize them by* when they return to become useful and hardworking members of society."

3. "You're not looking for anything. You're digging to build character. It's just if you find anything, the Warden would like to know about it."

4. "I want you to carry me up the mountain. I want to drink from the stream, and I want you to sing the song to me."

5. "If you must know," said _____, "I liked it better when you smoked."

6. "I can fix that."

7. "Well, then you'll have to hang me, too," said _____. "Because I kissed him back."

8. "I don't know what happened to my mother," _____ said. "She left and never came back."

9. "If only, if only, the moon speaks no reply;
Reflecting the sun and all that's gone by.
Be strong my weary wolf, turn around boldly.
Fly high, my baby bird,
My angel, my only."

Multiple Choice Unit Test #2 - **Holes** - page 4

IV. Vocabulary (Matching)

1.	feeble	A.	spread out in straggling or disordered fashion
2.	lopsided	B.	dangerously lacking in security or stability
3.	protruding	C.	area of authority or control
4.	engraved	D.	carved, cut, etched into something
5.	comprehend	E.	not giving up
6.	barren	F.	not able to be explained or interpreted
7.	precarious	G.	uncultivated or desolate country
8.	inexplicable	H.	sticking, jutting out
9.	jurisdiction	I.	being disgraced
10.	loot	J.	absurd, ridiculous
11.	wasteland	K.	heavier, larger on one side than on the other
12.	humiliating	L.	something illusory, deceptive
13.	refuge	M.	sterile, dull, unfruitful
14.	preposterous	N.	twisted, squirmed
15.	concoctions	O.	in terror of, anticipated with fear, alarm, reluctance
16.	mirage	P.	preparations made by mixing ingredients
17.	perseverance	Q.	stolen goods
18.	sprawled	R.	protection or shelter
19.	writhed	S.	lacking strength
20.	dread	T.	understand

Answer Sheet- Holes
Multiple Choice Unit Tests

Matching	Multiple Choice	Quotations (test #2)	Vocabulary	
1. _____	1. _____	1. _____	1. _____	11. _____
2. _____	2. _____	2. _____	2. _____	12. _____
3. _____	3. _____	3. _____	3. _____	13. _____
4. _____	4. _____	4. _____	4. _____	14. _____
5. _____	5. _____	5. _____	5. _____	15. _____
6. _____	6. _____	6. _____	6. _____	16. _____
7. _____	7. _____	7. _____	7. _____	17. _____
8. _____	8. _____	8. _____	8. _____	18. _____
	9. _____	9. _____	9. _____	19. _____
	10. _____	10. _____	10. _____	20. _____

Essay (test #1):

Answer Sheet Key - Holes
Multiple Choice Unit Tests

MC #1

Matching	Multiple Choice	Essay	Vocabulary	
1 C	1 d	Subjective	1 G	11 S
2 D	2 a		2 E	12 B
3 F	3 b		3 I	13 R
4 G	4 c		4 J	14 D
5 B	5 b		5 A	15 K
6 H	6 a		6 M	16 L
7 E	7 b		7 O	17 H
8 A	8 b		8 N	18 T
	9 d		9 P	19 F
	10 d		10 Q	20 C

MC #2

Matching	Multiple Choice	Quotations	Vocabulary	
1 E	1 c	1 B	1 S	11 G
2 F	2 c	2 E	2 K	12 I
3 A	3 b	3 E	3 H	13 R
4 D	4 b	4 H	4 D	14 J
5 B	5 c	5 F	5 T	15 P
6 G	6 c	6 D	6 M	16 L
7 H	7 c	7 G	7 B	17 E
8 C	8 d	8 C	8 F	18 A
	9 d	9 A	9 C	19 N
	10 c		10 Q	20 O

UNIT RESOURCE MATERIALS

Bulletin Board Ideas - Holes

1. See the bulletin board activity in Lesson One.

2. Get students to cut out pictures from magazines and newspapers that show people together and sharing and others that show aloneness. Stress that it is possible to feel very alone and still be together with other people.

3. Do a bulletin board activity about jobs in the juvenile justice field.

4. Gather pictures featuring an older person and a younger one. Try to get students to articulate what the relationship might be between the two. Is one perhaps serving in a mentor/counselor role?

5. Get students to look for (or draw) pictures of someone who reminds them of Stanley Yelnats. Tell them to be prepared to tell the class why the person in the pictures makes them think of Stanley.

6. Get students to write and post on the board very brief advertising for **Holes**. They might just want to write one- and two-liners.

7. Get students to write fan mail to Louis Sachar, and post the half dozen best results on the board.

8. Have students play a nickname game: each student posts on the board what he or she would choose as a nickname. Let other classmates try to figure out which nickname goes with which student. (Just be as sensitive as possible toward students who might find this activity embarrassing and not want to engage in it.)

9. Have students write and post on the board some reviews of **Holes**. Allow them to be as honest as they choose.

Extra Activities - Holes

One of the difficulties in teaching a novel is that not all students read at the same speed. One student who likes to read may take the book home and finish it in a day or two. Sometimes a few students finish the in-class assignments early. The problem, then, is finding suitable extra activities for students.

One thing that helps is to keep a little library in the classroom. For this unit on **Holes**, you might check out from the school library other books by Louis Sachar. A biography of the author would be interesting for some students. You may include other related books and articles that focus on some aspect of juvenile detention, friendship, personal courage, intrigue–whatever you and your students find interesting in light of your reading of **Holes**.

Other things you may keep on hand are puzzles. Some puzzles relating directly to **Holes** follow this page in your LitPlan.

Some students may like to draw, to sing, to dance, to paint, or participate in some other artistic endeavor. You might devise a contest or allow some extra-credit grade for your more artistic students. Note, too, that whatever students present might be used as bulletin board materials in the future. Check to see if students prefer to keep their artistic work; many will be persuaded to participate because they like the "immortality" they will achieve with future classes of students who use their classroom.

The pages which follow contain games, puzzles, and worksheets. The keys, when appropriate, immediately follow the puzzle or worksheet. There are two main groups of activities: one group for the unit; that is, generally relating to the **Holes** text, and another group of activities related strictly to vocabulary.

Directions for the games, puzzles, and worksheets are self-explanatory. The object here is to provide you with extra materials you may use in any way you choose.

More Activities - Holes

1. Have students write an epilogue to **Holes**, in which Stanley leaves Camp Green Lake but Zero has to stay behind.

2. Have students think about what Camp Green Lake would be like if all of the "inmates" there were girls. Have them describe the girls and their possible nicknames.

3. Have students do a brief writeup on what each of the camp's "inmates" might be doing professionally as adults.

4. Have students write brief newspaper accounts about what Stanley's lawyer and the Texas Attorney General found at Camp Green Lake. Who might be interviewed for such a story? What might they say?

5. Have students brainstorm in groups about an alternative title for the novel. What might it be called if it weren't called **Holes**? Get the students to explain why they would choose the other title.

6. If you have students who are artistically talented, you might have them write a short musical piece, write a song, or choreograph a dance sequence based on one episode/aspect of **Holes**. The artistic rendering could then be performed for the whole class.

7. Have students write "customer reviews" like the ones that appear on web sites for book sellers. The reviews need only be a paragraph or so long.

8. Have students discuss and then write briefly about what they would do were they to find a million dollars. What would they do with that much money?

9. Have students brainstorm about alternative nicknames for the characters in **Holes**. They should be able to tell why they chose the alternatives.

10. Have students write brief obituaries, one for Katherine Barlow and one for Sam the Onion Man.

Holes Word List

No.	Word	Clue/Definition
1.	BARLOW	Katherine's last name
2.	BASEBALL	Game Clyde Livingston played
3.	BOAT	Zero hid under it.
4.	CAVEMAN	Stanley's nickname
5.	DONKEY	Original Mary Lou was Sam's ___.
6.	ELYA	Stanley's great-great-grandfather
7.	FEET	Sweet ___; Clyde's nickname
8.	GREEN	Camp ___ Lake
9.	GYPSY	A one-legged one put a curse on the family
10.	HECTOR	Zero's real name
11.	HOLES	Title of the book
12.	JEWELS	These were in the suitcase Stanley & Zero found.
13.	LAUGHING	Miss Barlow was doing this when she died.
14.	LIPSTICK	Stanley found a ___ tube in the hole he dug.
15.	LIZARDS	Dangerous, yellow-spotted ones inhabited the area.
16.	LOU	Sam's boat: Mary ___
17.	MOM	Mr. Pendanski's nickname
18.	ONIONS	Sam offered these as a remedy.
19.	ONLY	Lullaby: If ___; if ___.
20.	PEACHES	Katherine made these.
21.	PENDANSKI	Name of the counselor
22.	READ	What Zero could not do
23.	RED	Color of Warden's hair and nails
24.	SACHAR	Author
25.	SEEDS	Mr. Sir ate sunflower ___.
26.	SHOVEL	Digging utensil
27.	SIR	He referred to a Girl Scout camp: Mr. ___
28.	SPAT	What each boy did when he finished digging his hole
29.	SPLOOSH	Zero drank it.
30.	TEACHER	Katherine Barlow's original profession
31.	THUMBS	Signal Stanley & Zero gave: ___ up
32.	VENOM	Ingredient in Warden's nail polish
33.	WARDEN	Woman who ran the camp
34.	WATER	Kind of truck Stanley stole and wrecked
35.	WRECK	Sign on the rec room door: ____ Room
36.	YELNATS	Stanley's last name
37.	ZERO	He escaped from the camp before Stanley did.
38.	ZERONI	Madame who was a one-legged Gypsy
39.	ZIGZAG	Zero attacked him when he started to beat Stanley.

WORD SEARCH - Holes

```
P M S B O N I O N S S Z I G Z A G L L Q
E C F A R K G H V L E X S Z Q R R A I V
N G L S L Q X C E S L S X F Q J M U P N
D R Q E F J N W K P O H B X G N D G S L
A B Y B B J E C R L H Q W P F R T H T D
N M B A M J Z Z N R C S K Q Y W X I I W
S B G L Q P X R T M F B V H P Z W N C H
K M R L F T R S F C K L M Y C H G G K K
I T H S V B R J Z H X H B W N K T W C H
D Y K R K S T Y N D B M H H J D N G R M
K F C B R P C H V C Q P F X P J H Y N S
D D Z K B X E L C S L W S T B W E H K Y
C W L T S B R A R N A V L M S L M P M C
D N A W F H W Y C J P C G Y N M G V C B
A W K R N J O J G H K R H A L Y B D A Q
E Y L E D D L V R W E I T A S A B N V T
R E H C A E T S E E D S Y P R O T C E H
K E G K M H N L E L O L Y L A A E F M R
B J D O U H Y V N Z N G O T P D E P A L
H D N M K A Y R Z O K W L S C T F Q N M
V E B W A T E R E P E J O S P L O O S H
V S B P V L X S R B Y N U G F R G L R H
L I Z A R D S T O Z E R O N I M O M L B
```

BARLOW	GYPSY	MOM	SEEDS	WARDEN
BASEBALL	HECTOR	ONIONS	SHOVEL	WATER
BOAT	HOLES	ONLY	SIR	WRECK
CAVEMAN	JEWELS	PEACHES	SPAT	YELNATS
DONKEY	LAUGHING	PENDANSKI	SPLOOSH	ZERO
ELYA	LIPSTICK	READ	TEACHER	ZERONI
FEET	LIZARDS	RED	THUMBS	ZIGZAG
GREEN	LOU	SACHAR	VENOM	

WORD SEARCH ANSWER KEY - Holes

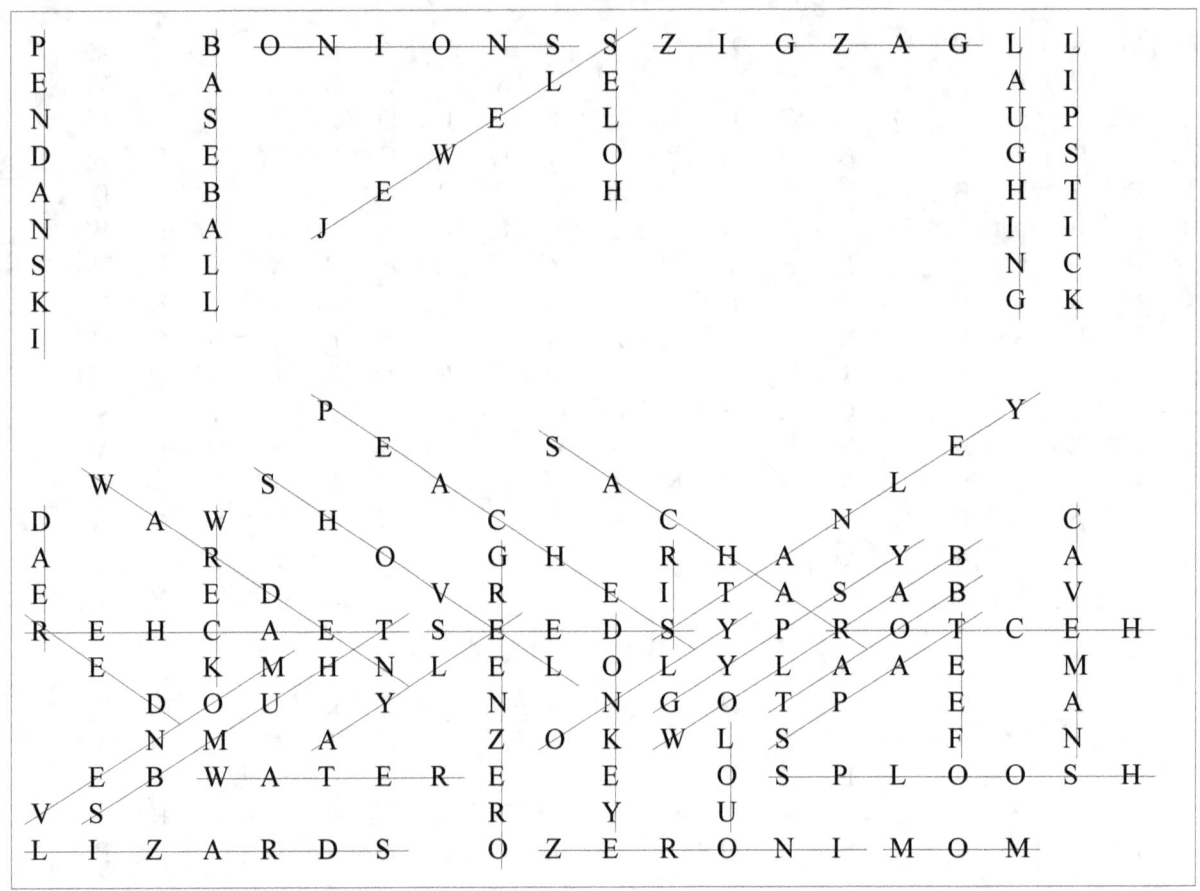

BARLOW	GYPSY	MOM	SEEDS	WARDEN
BASEBALL	HECTOR	ONIONS	SHOVEL	WATER
BOAT	HOLES	ONLY	SIR	WRECK
CAVEMAN	JEWELS	PEACHES	SPAT	YELNATS
DONKEY	LAUGHING	PENDANSKI	SPLOOSH	ZERO
ELYA	LIPSTICK	READ	TEACHER	ZERONI
FEET	LIZARDS	RED	THUMBS	ZIGZAG
GREEN	LOU	SACHAR	VENOM	

CROSSWORD - Holes

Across
2. A one-legged one put a curse on the family
5. Mr. Sir ate sunflower ___.
7. Dangerous, yellow-spotted ones inhabited the area.
10. Lullaby: If ___; if ___.
11. Stanley's nickname
13. Zero hid under it.
15. What each boy did when he finished digging his hole
16. These were in the suitcase Stanley & Zero found.
19. Katherine's last name
21. Signal Stanley & Zero gave: ___ up
22. Stanley's last name
23. Camp ___ Lake

Down
1. Sweet ___; Clyde's nickname
3. He referred to a Girl Scout camp: Mr. ___
4. Stanley's great-great-grandfather
5. Digging utensil
6. Title of the book
8. He escaped from the camp before Stanley did.
9. Author
10. Sam offered these as a remedy.
12. Mr. Pendanski's nickname
13. Game Clyde Livingston played
14. Original Mary Lou was Sam's ___.
17. Kind of truck Stanley stole and wrecked
18. Sam's boat: Mary ___
20. What Zero could not do

CROSSWORD ANSWER KEY - Holes

							1 F			
	2 G	Y	P	3 S	Y		E			
	4 E			I		5 S	E	E	D	6 H
7 L	I	8 Z	A	R	9 S		H		T	O
	Y	E			A		O		10 O N L Y	
	A	R		11 C	A	V	E	12 M	A	N E
		13 B	O	A	T		H	O	I	S
14 D		A			A		L	M		O
O		15 S	P	A	T	R		O		N
N		E			16 J	E	17 W	E	18 L	S
K	19 B	A	20 R	L	O	W		A		O
E	A		E				21 T	H	U	M B S
22 Y	E	L	N	A	T	S		E		
	L		D			23 G	R	E	E	N

Across
2. A one-legged one put a curse on the family
5. Mr. Sir ate sunflower ___.
7. Dangerous, yellow-spotted ones inhabited the area.
10. Lullaby: If ___; if ___.
11. Stanley's nickname
13. Zero hid under it.
15. What each boy did when he finished digging his hole
16. These were in the suitcase Stanley & Zero found.
19. Katherine's last name
21. Signal Stanley & Zero gave: ___ up
22. Stanley's last name
23. Camp ___ Lake

Down
1. Sweet ___; Clyde's nickname
3. He referred to a Girl Scout camp: Mr. ___
4. Stanley's great-great-grandfather
5. Digging utensil
6. Title of the book
8. He escaped from the camp before Stanley did.
9. Author
10. Sam offered these as a remedy.
12. Mr. Pendanski's nickname
13. Game Clyde Livingston played
14. Original Mary Lou was Sam's ___.
17. Kind of truck Stanley stole and wrecked
18. Sam's boat: Mary ___
20. What Zero could not do

MATCHING 1 - Holes

___ 1. VENOM   A. Sam's boat: Mary ___
___ 2. HOLES   B. Madame who was a one-legged Gypsy
___ 3. SHOVEL   C. Game Clyde Livingston played
___ 4. LAUGHING   D. Stanley's last name
___ 5. BARLOW   E. Digging utensil
___ 6. BASEBALL   F. Katherine Barlow's original profession
___ 7. BOAT   G. Title of the book
___ 8. SEEDS   H. Sam offered these as a remedy.
___ 9. READ   I. Sign on the rec room door: ____ Room
___10. PEACHES   J. Ingredient in Warden's nail polish
___11. WATER   K. Zero attacked him when he started to beat Stanley.
___12. TEACHER   L. He referred to a Girl Scout camp: Mr. ___
___13. ONIONS   M. What Zero could not do
___14. PENDANSKI   N. Miss Barlow was doing this when she died.
___15. ZERONI   O. Zero hid under it.
___16. ZIGZAG   P. A one-legged one put a curse on the family
___17. DONKEY   Q. Name of the counselor
___18. WARDEN   R. Mr. Sir ate sunflower ___.
___19. HECTOR   S. Zero's real name
___20. LOU   T. Katherine's last name
___21. GYPSY   U. Color of Warden's hair and nails
___22. YELNATS   V. Original Mary Lou was Sam's ___.
___23. SIR   W. Kind of truck Stanley stole and wrecked
___24. WRECK   X. Katherine made these.
___25. RED   Y. Woman who ran the camp

MATCHING 1 ANSWER KEY - Holes

J - 1. VENOM	A.	Sam's boat: Mary ___
G - 2. HOLES	B.	Madame who was a one-legged Gypsy
E - 3. SHOVEL	C.	Game Clyde Livingston played
N - 4. LAUGHING	D.	Stanley's last name
T - 5. BARLOW	E.	Digging utensil
C - 6. BASEBALL	F.	Katherine Barlow's original profession
O - 7. BOAT	G.	Title of the book
R - 8. SEEDS	H.	Sam offered these as a remedy.
M - 9. READ	I.	Sign on the rec room door: ___ Room
X - 10. PEACHES	J.	Ingredient in Warden's nail polish
W - 11. WATER	K.	Zero attacked him when he started to beat Stanley.
F - 12. TEACHER	L.	He referred to a Girl Scout camp: Mr. ___
H - 13. ONIONS	M.	What Zero could not do
Q - 14. PENDANSKI	N.	Miss Barlow was doing this when she died.
B - 15. ZERONI	O.	Zero hid under it.
K - 16. ZIGZAG	P.	A one-legged one put a curse on the family
V - 17. DONKEY	Q.	Name of the counselor
Y - 18. WARDEN	R.	Mr. Sir ate sunflower ___.
S - 19. HECTOR	S.	Zero's real name
A - 20. LOU	T.	Katherine's last name
P - 21. GYPSY	U.	Color of Warden's hair and nails
D - 22. YELNATS	V.	Original Mary Lou was Sam's ___.
L - 23. SIR	W.	Kind of truck Stanley stole and wrecked
I - 24. WRECK	X.	Katherine made these.
U - 25. RED	Y.	Woman who ran the camp

MATCHING 2 - Holes

___ 1. BASEBALL   A. What each boy did when he finished digging his hole

___ 2. ZERO   B. Madame who was a one-legged Gypsy

___ 3. FEET   C. Sam offered these as a remedy.

___ 4. ONLY   D. Name of the counselor

___ 5. WARDEN   E. Sign on the rec room door: ___ Room

___ 6. SPAT   F. Katherine made these.

___ 7. PEACHES   G. Lullaby: If ___; if ___.

___ 8. CAVEMAN   H. Miss Barlow was doing this when she died.

___ 9. PENDANSKI   I. Color of Warden's hair and nails

___ 10. LAUGHING   J. He referred to a Girl Scout camp: Mr. ___

___ 11. RED   K. Sam's boat: Mary ___

___ 12. LOU   L. Kind of truck Stanley stole and wrecked

___ 13. ELYA   M. Signal Stanley & Zero gave: ___ up

___ 14. WRECK   N. What Zero could not do

___ 15. ONIONS   O. Title of the book

___ 16. THUMBS   P. Game Clyde Livingston played

___ 17. ZERONI   Q. Stanley found a ___ tube in the hole he dug.

___ 18. WATER   R. Woman who ran the camp

___ 19. READ   S. Katherine's last name

___ 20. BARLOW   T. Sweet ___; Clyde's nickname

___ 21. HOLES   U. He escaped from the camp before Stanley did.

___ 22. SEEDS   V. Stanley's nickname

___ 23. LIZARDS   W. Mr. Sir ate sunflower ___.

___ 24. LIPSTICK   X. Dangerous, yellow-spotted ones inhabited the area.

___ 25. SIR   Y. Stanley's great-great-grandfather

MATCHING 2 ANSWER KEY - Holes

P - 1. BASEBALL	A.	What each boy did when he finished digging his hole
U - 2. ZERO	B.	Madame who was a one-legged Gypsy
T - 3. FEET	C.	Sam offered these as a remedy.
G - 4. ONLY	D.	Name of the counselor
R - 5. WARDEN	E.	Sign on the rec room door: ___ Room
A - 6. SPAT	F.	Katherine made these.
F - 7. PEACHES	G.	Lullaby: If ___; if ___.
V - 8. CAVEMAN	H.	Miss Barlow was doing this when she died.
D - 9. PENDANSKI	I.	Color of Warden's hair and nails
H -10. LAUGHING	J.	He referred to a Girl Scout camp: Mr. ___
I -11. RED	K.	Sam's boat: Mary ___
K -12. LOU	L.	Kind of truck Stanley stole and wrecked
Y -13. ELYA	M.	Signal Stanley & Zero gave: ___ up
E -14. WRECK	N.	What Zero could not do
C -15. ONIONS	O.	Title of the book
M -16. THUMBS	P.	Game Clyde Livingston played
B -17. ZERONI	Q.	Stanley found a ___ tube in the hole he dug.
L -18. WATER	R.	Woman who ran the camp
N -19. READ	S.	Katherine's last name
S -20. BARLOW	T.	Sweet ___; Clyde's nickname
O -21. HOLES	U.	He escaped from the camp before Stanley did.
W 22. SEEDS	V.	Stanley's nickname
X -23. LIZARDS	W.	Mr. Sir ate sunflower ___.
Q -24. LIPSTICK	X.	Dangerous, yellow-spotted ones inhabited the area.
J - 25. SIR	Y.	Stanley's great-great-grandfather

JUGGLE LETTER 1 - Holes

1. TPAS = 1. _____
   What each boy did when he finished digging his hole

2. EVACMNA = 2. _____
   Stanley's nickname

3. ISR = 3. _____
   He referred to a Girl Scout camp: Mr. ___

4. DRNWEA = 4. _____
   Woman who ran the camp

5. DSLRIAZ = 5. _____
   Dangerous, yellow-spotted ones inhabited the area.

6. SLOSOPH = 6. _____
   Zero drank it.

7. DSESE = 7. _____
   Mr. Sir ate sunflower ___.

8. PYSGY = 8. _____
   A one-legged one put a curse on the family

9. REIZNO = 9. _____
   Madame who was a one-legged Gypsy

10. AEDR =10. _____
    What Zero could not do

11. EVNMO =11. _____
    Ingredient in Warden's nail polish

12. ERD =12. _____
    Color of Warden's hair and nails

13. BOAT =13. _____
    Zero hid under it.

14. EKWRC =14. _____
    Sign on the rec room door: ____ Room

15. CARSAH =15. _____
    Author

16. UGHNILGA =16. _____
Miss Barlow was doing this when she died.

17. OYLN =17. _____
Lullaby: If ___; if ___.

18. HESVLO =18. _____
Digging utensil

19. RLOBAW =19. _____
Katherine's last name

20. HESOL =20. _____
Title of the book

JUGGLE LETTER 1 ANSWER KEY - Holes

1. TPAS = 1. SPAT
What each boy did when he finished digging his hole

2. EVACMNA = 2. CAVEMAN
Stanley's nickname

3. ISR = 3. SIR
He referred to a Girl Scout camp: Mr. ___

4. DRNWEA = 4. WARDEN
Woman who ran the camp

5. DSLRIAZ = 5. LIZARDS
Dangerous, yellow-spotted ones inhabited the area.

6. SLOSOPH = 6. SPLOOSH
Zero drank it.

7. DSESE = 7. SEEDS
Mr. Sir ate sunflower ___.

8. PYSGY = 8. GYPSY
A one-legged one put a curse on the family

9. REIZNO = 9. ZERONI
Madame who was a one-legged Gypsy

10. AEDR =10. READ
What Zero could not do

11. EVNMO =11. VENOM
Ingredient in Warden's nail polish

12. ERD =12. RED
Color of Warden's hair and nails

13. BOAT =13. BOAT
Zero hid under it.

14. EKWRC =14. WRECK
Sign on the rec room door: ___ Room

15. CARSAH =15. SACHAR
Author

16. UGHNILGA =16. LAUGHING

Miss Barlow was doing this when she died.

17. OYLN =17. ONLY

Lullaby: If ___; if ___.

18. HESVLO =18. SHOVEL

Digging utensil

19. RLOBAW =19. BARLOW

Katherine's last name

20. HESOL =20. HOLES

Title of the book

JUGGLE LETTER 2 - Holes

1. HCEASPE = 1. _____
   Katherine made these.

2. LYEA = 2. _____
   Stanley's great-great-grandfather

3. TEEF = 3. _____
   Sweet ___; Clyde's nickname

4. AREWT = 4. _____
   Kind of truck Stanley stole and wrecked

5. ONOINS = 5. _____
   Sam offered these as a remedy.

6. ORZE = 6. _____
   He escaped from the camp before Stanley did.

7. EEHATCR = 7. _____
   Katherine Barlow's original profession

8. LBSLEAAB = 8. _____
   Game Clyde Livingston played

9. NDEANKSPI = 9. _____
   Name of the counselor

10. GIGZZA =10. _____
    Zero attacked him when he started to beat Stanley.

11. EEWJLS =11. _____
    These were in the suitcase Stanley & Zero found.

12. YKODEN =12. _____
    Original Mary Lou was Sam's ___.

13. OMM =13. _____
    Mr. Pendanski's nickname

14. OCRHET =14. _____
    Zero's real name

15. EERGN =15. _____
    Camp ___ Lake

16. AYSLTEN   =16. _____
                Stanley's last name

17. SHBMUT   =17. _____
                Signal Stanley & Zero gave: ___ up

18. UOL   =18. _____
                Sam's boat: Mary ___

19. ICLKSTPI   =19. _____
                Stanley found a ___ tube in the hole he dug.

JUGGLE LETTER 2 ANSWER KEY - Holes

1. HCEASPE = 1. PEACHES
   Katherine made these.

2. LYEA = 2. ELYA
   Stanley's great-great-grandfather

3. TEEF = 3. FEET
   Sweet ___; Clyde's nickname

4. AREWT = 4. WATER
   Kind of truck Stanley stole and wrecked

5. ONOINS = 5. ONIONS
   Sam offered these as a remedy.

6. ORZE = 6. ZERO
   He escaped from the camp before Stanley did.

7. EEHATCR = 7. TEACHER
   Katherine Barlow's original profession

8. LBSLEAAB = 8. BASEBALL
   Game Clyde Livingston played

9. NDEANKSPI = 9. PENDANSKI
   Name of the counselor

10. GIGZZA =10. ZIGZAG
    Zero attacked him when he started to beat Stanley.

11. EEWJLS =11. JEWELS
    These were in the suitcase Stanley & Zero found.

12. YKODEN =12. DONKEY
    Original Mary Lou was Sam's ___.

13. OMM =13. MOM
    Mr. Pendanski's nickname

14. OCRHET =14. HECTOR
    Zero's real name

15. EERGN =15. GREEN
    Camp ___ Lake

16. AYSLTEN =16. YELNATS

Stanley's last name

17. SHBMUT =17. THUMBS

Signal Stanley & Zero gave: ___ up

18. UOL =18. LOU

Sam's boat: Mary ___

19. ICLKSTPI =19. LIPSTICK

Stanley found a ___ tube in the hole he dug.

VOCABULARY RESOURCE MATERIALS

Holes Vocabulary Word List

No.	Word	Clue/Definition
1.	GROTESQUE	Outlandish; bizarre
2.	TEDIOUS	Tiresome; wearisome
3.	PROTECTED	Keep safe; guarded
4.	AWKWARD	Clumsy; unskillful
5.	TORMENT	Great pain or anguish
6.	DEFECTIVE	Flawed; doesn't work right
7.	FUGITIVE	Person running away from the law
8.	RATIO	Relation between two things
9.	HOVER	Floating or suspended in air
10.	GULLY	Deep ditch cut in the earth by running water
11.	THROBBING	Beating rapidly or violently; pounding
12.	VISIBLE	Able to be seen
13.	SPEWED	Forced out
14.	PREPOSTEROUS	Absurd; ridiculous
15.	FAMILIAR	Often encountered; known
16.	WASTELAND	Uncultivated or desolate country
17.	FEEBLE	Lacking strength
18.	FLINCH	Draw away from something surprising or painful
19.	EXHAUSTED	Very tired; weary
20.	DELIRIOUS	Mentally confused
21.	DRAWL	Speech characterized by lengthened, drawn-out vowels
22.	NECTAR	Delicious, invigorating drink
23.	INVESTIGATION	Systematic examination
24.	DESPICABLE	Vile; awful
25.	SUBTLE	So slight as to be difficult to distinguish
26.	EVAPORATED	Changed to vapor
27.	URGE	Force moving one to do something
28.	HUMILIATING	Embarrassing; being disgraced
29.	SUSPECT	Have doubts about; distrust
30.	PARCHED	Very dry
31.	RETRIEVED	Got back; regained
32.	CAUTIOUS	Careful
33.	REQUIREMENTS	Necessary things
34.	SCARCITY	Shortage
35.	FABULOUS	Barely believable; astonishing; amazing
36.	CERTAIN	Sure
37.	DESCENDANTS	Individuals from which others come; opposite of ancestors
38.	IMAGE	Reproduction of the form of something or someone
39.	CALLUSED	Having a thickening and hardness of skin
40.	VENTILATION	Admitting fresh air to replace stale air
41.	AMAZED	Filled with surprise; astonished

Holes Vocabulary Word List Continued

No.	Word	Clue/Definition
42.	PRECARIOUS	Dangerously lacking in security or stability
43.	SWISH	Move with a whistle or hiss
44.	LEGITIMATE	Lawful; legal
45.	LOGICAL	Consistent in reasoning
46.	ENGRAVED	Carved, cut, or etched into something
47.	DESOLATE	Dreary; unfit for habitation or use
48.	REFUGE	Place of protection or shelter
49.	MIRAGE	An illusion; something deceptive
50.	CONDEMNED	Found guilty
51.	SOGGY	Soaked with moisture
52.	STIFLING	Smothering; suffocating
53.	LOOT	Stolen goods
54.	DOOMED	Condemned to a severe penalty
55.	LOPSIDED	Heavier or larger on one side than the other
56.	APPRECIATE	Value
57.	PIG	Jargon formed by putting first consonant at the end of a word and adding a syllable: ___ Latin
58.	INCARCERATED	Shut in; confined--usually in jail
59.	MYSTERIOUS	Not fully understood
60.	INEXPLICABLE	Not able to be explained or interpreted
61.	VENOM	Poisonous secretion of an animal, such as a spider or snake
62.	PROTRUDING	Sticking out; jutting out
63.	HAZE	Moisture, dust, or vapor suspended in the air
64.	FOSSIL	Skeleton or imprint of an organism in a rock
65.	METALLIC	Like or containing a metal
66.	DREAD	Anticipate with fear, alarm, or reluctance
67.	IMPROVE	Get better
68.	JURISDICTION	Area of authority or control
69.	HITCHING	Hooking to; connecting
70.	SCORPION	Spider-like animal with a venomous tail
71.	FIERY	Very hot; like fire
72.	WRITHED	Twisted; squirmed
73.	BARREN	Sterile; dull; unfruitful
74.	SPRAWLED	Spread out in straggling or disorderly fashion
75.	WHEELBARROW	Vehicle with handles & a wheel used to convey loads by hand
76.	SUNDIAL	Instrument that indicates local solar time
77.	SHRANK	Got smaller
78.	STATIONERY	Writing paper and envelopes
79.	DELAYED	Put off until another time
80.	PERSEVERANCE	Not giving up

Holes Vocabulary Word List Continued

No.	Word	Clue/Definition
81.	PRECIPICE	Extremely steep or overhanging mass of rock
82.	INSISTS	Refuses to yield
83.	ADJACENT	Close together; next to
84.	INGREDIENT	Something that is an element; a part of
85.	COMPREHEND	Understand
86.	CURSES	Appeals for evil or injury to befall someone or something
87.	CONCOCTIONS	Preparations made by mixing ingredients

VOCABULARY WORD SEARCH - Holes

```
K N F H D D E S U L L A C S W I S H A D
V E O D R E F F A M I L I A R X B K M F
Z C S C A S S Z N Y F P K C U M S D A R
X T S M W P H S A X W M R B L T N B Z B
R A I S L I S D P Y Y E V O N D I T E S
E R L D C C J V I G Z W H E T R C O D J
L O G I C A L E G A R I M A G E G R U K
B R S D C B R O H I B E P E P A C A N S
I V W E Y L S C T F R C T S T D P T L C
S S N R R E C H I I S A U R C A L I E S
I T E L B E E F U T L S H S I D L O Y D
V I R W R D H Q S O Y O U C E E V L O Q
F F R T P Z E I S Y V O P L X N V C I T
P L A G C R S E L C L E W S E M D E Y C
L I B M R N D L S U U A N X I E E K D Y
N N M E I O U R B U R R H O L D W Y R J
Y G V P Y G T A E P B A S I M N E S A D
L O D B R R F E S F U T R E R O P D W P
H D E M O O D C S S U I L X S C S H K W
F U G I T I V E T Q O G N E Z F F N W N
E V I T C E F E D U U T E D I O U S A D
S H R A N K D C S W H E E L B A R R O W
P R E C A R I O U S C O R P I O N N B L
```

ADJACENT	DREAD	LOGICAL	SHRANK
AMAZED	EXHAUSTED	LOOT	SOGGY
AWKWARD	FABULOUS	LOPSIDED	SPEWED
BARREN	FAMILIAR	METALLIC	SPRAWLED
CALLUSED	FEEBLE	MIRAGE	STIFLING
CAUTIOUS	FIERY	NECTAR	SUBTLE
CERTAIN	FOSSIL	PIG	SUSPECT
CONDEMNED	FUGITIVE	PRECARIOUS	SWISH
CURSES	GROTESQUE	PROTECTED	TEDIOUS
DEFECTIVE	GULLY	RATIO	URGE
DELIRIOUS	HAZE	REFUGE	VENOM
DESOLATE	HOVER	REQUIREMENTS	VISIBLE
DESPICABLE	IMAGE	RETRIEVED	WHEELBARROW
DOOMED	IMPROVE	SCARCITY	WRITHED
DRAWL	INSISTS	SCORPION	

VOCABULARY WORD SEARCH ANSWER KEY - Holes

ADJACENT	DREAD	LOGICAL	SHRANK
AMAZED	EXHAUSTED	LOOT	SOGGY
AWKWARD	FABULOUS	LOPSIDED	SPEWED
BARREN	FAMILIAR	METALLIC	SPRAWLED
CALLUSED	FEEBLE	MIRAGE	STIFLING
CAUTIOUS	FIERY	NECTAR	SUBTLE
CERTAIN	FOSSIL	PIG	SUSPECT
CONDEMNED	FUGITIVE	PRECARIOUS	SWISH
CURSES	GROTESQUE	PROTECTED	TEDIOUS
DEFECTIVE	GULLY	RATIO	URGE
DELIRIOUS	HAZE	REFUGE	VENOM
DESOLATE	HOVER	REQUIREMENTS	VISIBLE
DESPICABLE	IMAGE	RETRIEVED	WHEELBARROW
DOOMED	IMPROVE	SCARCITY	WRITHED
DRAWL	INSISTS	SCORPION	

VOCABULARY CROSSWORD - Holes

Across
4. Floating or suspended in air
6. Relation between two things
8. Deep ditch cut in the earth by running water
9. Reproduction of the form of something or someone
10. Often encountered; known
12. Great pain or anguish
15. Outlandish; bizarre
17. Jargon formed by putting first consonant at the end of a word and adding a syllable: ___ Latin
18. Move with a whistle or hiss
19. So slight as to be difficult to distinguish
20. Have doubts about; distrust

Down
1. Place of protection or shelter
2. Force moving one to do something
3. Able to be seen
5. Poisonous secretion of an animal, such as a spider or snake
7. Clumsy; unskillful
10. Person running away from the law
11. Refuses to yield
12. Tiresome; wearisome
13. Delicious, invigorating drink
14. Consistent in reasoning
16. Forced out

VOCABULARY CROSSWORD ANSWER KEY - Holes

										1 R	
		2 U				3 V				E	
4 H	5 O	V	E	R		6 R	7 A	T	I	O	F
	E	8 G	U	L	L	Y	W		S		U
	N	E				K	9 I	M	A	G	E
	O					W	B			E	
10 F	A	M	I	11 L	I	A	R			L	
U				N		12 T	O	R	13 M	E	N	T	14 L
15 G	R	O	T	E	S	Q	U	E		D			16 S	O
I				I			D			C		17 P	I	G
T		18 S	W	I	S	H		19 I	S	U	B	T	L	E
I				T				O			A		W	C
V				S				U			R		E	A
E				20 S	U	S	P	E	C	T			D	L

Across
4. Floating or suspended in air
6. Relation between two things
8. Deep ditch cut in the earth by running water
9. Reproduction of the form of something or someone
10. Often encountered; known
12. Great pain or anguish
15. Outlandish; bizarre
17. Jargon formed by putting first consonant at the end of a word and adding a syllable: ___ Latin
18. Move with a whistle or hiss
19. So slight as to be difficult to distinguish
20. Have doubts about; distrust

Down
1. Place of protection or shelter
2. Force moving one to do something
3. Able to be seen
5. Poisonous secretion of an animal, such as a spider or snake
7. Clumsy; unskillful
10. Person running away from the law
11. Refuses to yield
12. Tiresome; wearisome
13. Delicious, invigorating drink
14. Consistent in reasoning
16. Forced out

VOCABULARY MATCHING 1 - Holes

___ 1. RETRIEVED　　A. Not able to be explained or interpreted

___ 2. HAZE　　B. Shortage

___ 3. DESPICABLE　　C. Value

___ 4. REFUGE　　D. Not giving up

___ 5. NECTAR　　E. Great pain or anguish

___ 6. REQUIREMENTS　　F. Sure

___ 7. TORMENT　　G. Extremely steep or overhanging mass of rock

___ 8. INEXPLICABLE　　H. Changed to vapor

___ 9. VENTILATION　　I. Admitting fresh air to replace stale air

___ 10. PERSEVERANCE　　J. Place of protection or shelter

___ 11. LOOT　　K. Stolen goods

___ 12. FEEBLE　　L. Carved, cut, or etched into something

___ 13. ENGRAVED　　M. Anticipate with fear, alarm, or reluctance

___ 14. BARREN　　N. Lacking strength

___ 15. PRECIPICE　　O. Have doubts about; distrust

___ 16. INGREDIENT　　P. Mentally confused

___ 17. DELIRIOUS　　Q. Sterile; dull; unfruitful

___ 18. APPRECIATE　　R. Got back; regained

___ 19. CURSES　　S. Moisture, dust, or vapor suspended in the air

___ 20. SUSPECT　　T. Vile; awful

___ 21. EVAPORATED　　U. Delicious, invigorating drink

___ 22. SCARCITY　　V. Dangerously lacking in security or stability

___ 23. PRECARIOUS　　W. Necessary things

___ 24. CERTAIN　　X. Something that is an element; a part of

___ 25. DREAD　　Y. Appeals for evil or injury to befall someone or something

VOCABULARY MATCHING 1 ANSWER KEY - Holes

R - 1. RETRIEVED	A.	Not able to be explained or interpreted
S - 2. HAZE	B.	Shortage
T - 3. DESPICABLE	C.	Value
J - 4. REFUGE	D.	Not giving up
U - 5. NECTAR	E.	Great pain or anguish
W 6. REQUIREMENTS	F.	Sure
E - 7. TORMENT	G.	Extremely steep or overhanging mass of rock
A - 8. INEXPLICABLE	H.	Changed to vapor
I - 9. VENTILATION	I.	Admitting fresh air to replace stale air
D -10. PERSEVERANCE	J.	Place of protection or shelter
K -11. LOOT	K.	Stolen goods
N -12. FEEBLE	L.	Carved, cut, or etched into something
L -13. ENGRAVED	M.	Anticipate with fear, alarm, or reluctance
Q -14. BARREN	N.	Lacking strength
G -15. PRECIPICE	O.	Have doubts about; distrust
X -16. INGREDIENT	P.	Mentally confused
P -17. DELIRIOUS	Q.	Sterile; dull; unfruitful
C -18. APPRECIATE	R.	Got back; regained
Y -19. CURSES	S.	Moisture, dust, or vapor suspended in the air
O -20. SUSPECT	T.	Vile; awful
H -21. EVAPORATED	U.	Delicious, invigorating drink
B -22. SCARCITY	V.	Dangerously lacking in security or stability
V -23. PRECARIOUS	W.	Necessary things
F -24. CERTAIN	X.	Something that is an element; a part of
M 25. DREAD	Y.	Appeals for evil or injury to befall someone or something

VOCABULARY MATCHING 2 - Holes

___ 1. URGE A. Admitting fresh air to replace stale air
___ 2. REFUGE B. Preparations made by mixing ingredients
___ 3. LOPSIDED C. Sterile; dull; unfruitful
___ 4. JURISDICTION D. Place of protection or shelter
___ 5. FLINCH E. Consistent in reasoning
___ 6. SUBTLE F. Deep ditch cut in the earth by running water
___ 7. HUMILIATING G. Careful
___ 8. LOGICAL H. Smothering; suffocating
___ 9. CONCOCTIONS I. Very hot; like fire
___ 10. PREPOSTEROUS J. Shortage
___ 11. WHEELBARROW K. Absurd; ridiculous
___ 12. PRECIPICE L. Draw away from something surprising or painful
___ 13. PROTRUDING M. Force moving one to do something
___ 14. STIFLING N. Area of authority or control
___ 15. VENTILATION O. So slight as to be difficult to distinguish
___ 16. SOGGY P. Very tired; weary
___ 17. RATIO Q. Embarrassing; being disgraced
___ 18. FIERY R. Vehicle with handles & a wheel used to convey loads by hand
___ 19. EXHAUSTED S. Heavier or larger on one side than the other
___ 20. SCARCITY T. Relation between two things
___ 21. DEFECTIVE U. Sticking out; jutting out
___ 22. GULLY V. Extremely steep or overhanging mass of rock
___ 23. FOSSIL W. Flawed; doesn't work right
___ 24. BARREN X. Skeleton or imprint of an organism in a rock
___ 25. CAUTIOUS Y. Soaked with moisture

VOCABULARY MATCHING 2 ANWER KEY - Holes

M - 1. URGE		A. Admitting fresh air to replace stale air
D - 2. REFUGE		B. Preparations made by mixing ingredients
S - 3. LOPSIDED		C. Sterile; dull; unfruitful
N - 4. JURISDICTION		D. Place of protection or shelter
L - 5. FLINCH		E. Consistent in reasoning
O - 6. SUBTLE		F. Deep ditch cut in the earth by running water
Q - 7. HUMILIATING		G. Careful
E - 8. LOGICAL		H. Smothering; suffocating
B - 9. CONCOCTIONS		I. Very hot; like fire
K - 10. PREPOSTEROUS		J. Shortage
R - 11. WHEELBARROW		K. Absurd; ridiculous
V - 12. PRECIPICE		L. Draw away from something surprising or painful
U - 13. PROTRUDING		M. Force moving one to do something
H - 14. STIFLING		N. Area of authority or control
A - 15. VENTILATION		O. So slight as to be difficult to distinguish
Y - 16. SOGGY		P. Very tired; weary
T - 17. RATIO		Q. Embarrassing; being disgraced
I - 18. FIERY		R. Vehicle with handles & a wheel used to convey loads by hand
P - 19. EXHAUSTED		S. Heavier or larger on one side than the other
J - 20. SCARCITY		T. Relation between two things
W 21. DEFECTIVE		U. Sticking out; jutting out
F - 22. GULLY		V. Extremely steep or overhanging mass of rock
X - 23. FOSSIL		W. Flawed; doesn't work right
C - 24. BARREN		X. Skeleton or imprint of an organism in a rock
G - 25. CAUTIOUS		Y. Soaked with moisture

VOCABLUARY JUGGLE LETTER 1 - Holes

1. EGTIIDNREN = 1. _____
   Something that is an element; a part of

2. AWKDWAR = 2. _____
   Clumsy; unskillful

3. EILSPDDO = 3. _____
   Heavier or larger on one side than the other

4. OCTIOCNSNCO = 4. _____
   Preparations made by mixing ingredients

5. OUSTSIMYRE = 5. _____
   Not fully understood

6. ALDRW = 6. _____
   Speech characterized by lengthened, drawn-out vowels

7. MEITEILTGA = 7. _____
   Lawful; legal

8. NREMOTT = 8. _____
   Great pain or anguish

9. OICTUSUA = 9. _____
   Careful

10. EEWDPS = 10. _____
    Forced out

11. ESSPURTROOEP = 11. _____
    Absurd; ridiculous

12. LCGOILA = 12. _____
    Consistent in reasoning

13. RMNECEDOHP = 13. _____
    Understand

14. BOUULAFS = 14. _____
    Barely believable; astonishing; amazing

15. LSIOSF = 15. _____
    Skeleton or imprint of an organism in a rock

16. UIDJNSICOIRT   =16. _____
                        Area of authority or control

17. AELNASWDT   =17. _____
                        Uncultivated or desolate country

18. LORDIIUES   =18. _____
                        Mentally confused

19. EODMOD   =19. _____
                        Condemned to a severe penalty

20. SOIDTUE   =20. _____
                        Tiresome; wearisome

21. NJDECAAT   =21. _____
                        Close together; next to

22. GRUE   =22. _____
                        Force moving one to do something

23. AOVDERTPAE   =23. _____
                        Changed to vapor

24. REUSSC   =24. _____
                        Appeals for evil or injury to befall someone or something

25. MIEAG   =25. _____
                        Reproduction of the form of something or someone

26. IRTUNRDGOP   =26. _____
                        Sticking out; jutting out

27. CADEHRP   =27. _____
                        Very dry

28. NEYOSRTIAT   =28. _____
                        Writing paper and envelopes

29. EEEFLB   =29. _____
                        Lacking strength

VOCABLUARY JUGGLE LETTER 1 ANSWER KEY - Holes

1. EGTIIDNREN = 1. INGREDIENT
   Something that is an element; a part of

2. AWKDWAR = 2. AWKWARD
   Clumsy; unskillful

3. EILSPDDO = 3. LOPSIDED
   Heavier or larger on one side than the other

4. OCTIOCNSNCO = 4. CONCOCTIONS
   Preparations made by mixing ingredients

5. OUSTSIMYRE = 5. MYSTERIOUS
   Not fully understood

6. ALDRW = 6. DRAWL
   Speech characterized by lengthened, drawn-out vowels

7. MEITEILTGA = 7. LEGITIMATE
   Lawful; legal

8. NREMOTT = 8. TORMENT
   Great pain or anguish

9. OICTUSUA = 9. CAUTIOUS
   Careful

10. EEWDPS = 10. SPEWED
    Forced out

11. ESSPURTROOEP = 11. PREPOSTEROUS
    Absurd; ridiculous

12. LCGOILA = 12. LOGICAL
    Consistent in reasoning

13. RMNECEDOHP = 13. COMPREHEND
    Understand

14. BOUULAFS = 14. FABULOUS
    Barely believable; astonishing; amazing

15. LSIOSF = 15. FOSSIL
    Skeleton or imprint of an organism in a rock

16. UIDJNSICOIRT   =16. JURISDICTION
                    Area of authority or control

17. AELNASWDT   =17. WASTELAND
                    Uncultivated or desolate country

18. LORDIIUES   =18. DELIRIOUS
                    Mentally confused

19. EODMOD   =19. DOOMED
                    Condemned to a severe penalty

20. SOIDTUE   =20. TEDIOUS
                    Tiresome; wearisome

21. NJDECAAT   =21. ADJACENT
                    Close together; next to

22. GRUE   =22. URGE
                    Force moving one to do something

23. AOVDERTPAE   =23. EVAPORATED
                    Changed to vapor

24. REUSSC   =24. CURSES
                    Appeals for evil or injury to befall someone or something

25. MIEAG   =25. IMAGE
                    Reproduction of the form of something or someone

26. IRTUNRDGOP   =26. PROTRUDING
                    Sticking out; jutting out

27. CADEHRP   =27. PARCHED
                    Very dry

28. NEYOSRTIAT   =28. STATIONERY
                    Writing paper and envelopes

29. EEEFLB   =29. FEEBLE
                    Lacking strength

VOCABLUARY JUGGLE LETTER 2 - Holes

1. VSERCERAENEP = 1. _____
   Not giving up

2. GIP = 2. _____
   Jargon formed by putting first consonant at the end of a word and adding a syllable: ___ Latin

3. ELPSWARD = 3. _____
   Spread out in straggling or disorderly fashion

4. DSAUEXEHT = 4. _____
   Very tired; weary

5. LBIESVI = 5. _____
   Able to be seen

6. EATIRNC = 6. _____
   Sure

7. CCIRAYTS = 7. _____
   Shortage

8. OERCTPDET = 8. _____
   Keep safe; guarded

9. LAXIIBPECLNE = 9. _____
   Not able to be explained or interpreted

10. WSISH =10. _____
    Move with a whistle or hiss

11. MPRVEIO =11. _____
    Get better

12. IRUCREPOSA =12. _____
    Dangerously lacking in security or stability

13. LAEDOEST =13. _____
    Dreary; unfit for habitation or use

14. BNTHOIRGB =14. _____
    Beating rapidly or violently; pounding

15. ITNHCIHG =15. _____
    Hooking to; connecting

16. EVIONLTNIAT =16. _____
Admitting fresh air to replace stale air

17. RDEAVGEN =17. _____
Carved, cut, or etched into something

18. LTLIAECM =18. _____
Like or containing a metal

19. TUGVEFII =19. _____
Person running away from the law

20. ENRTCA =20. _____
Delicious, invigorating drink

21. NEMOV =21. _____
Poisonous secretion of an animal, such as a spider or snake

22. SNISTIS =22. _____
Refuses to yield

23. LYULG =23. _____
Deep ditch cut in the earth by running water

24. OLTO =24. _____
Stolen goods

25. EAYLDED =25. _____
Put off until another time

26. ZAHE =26. _____
Moisture, dust, or vapor suspended in the air

27. EVEDIRTER =27. _____
Got back; regained

28. HFINCL =28. _____
Draw away from something surprising or painful

29. EPEICRPCI =29. _____
Extremely steep or overhanging mass of rock

VOCABLUARY JUGGLE LETTER 2 ANSWER KEY - Holes

1. VSERCERAENEP = 1. PERSEVERANCE

    Not giving up

2. GIP = 2. PIG

    Jargon formed by putting first consonant at the end of a word and adding a syllable: ___ Latin

3. ELPSWARD = 3. SPRAWLED

    Spread out in straggling or disorderly fashion

4. DSAUEXEHT = 4. EXHAUSTED

    Very tired; weary

5. LBIESVI = 5. VISIBLE

    Able to be seen

6. EATIRNC = 6. CERTAIN

    Sure

7. CCIRAYTS = 7. SCARCITY

    Shortage

8. OERCTPDET = 8. PROTECTED

    Keep safe; guarded

9. LAXIIBPECLNE = 9. INEXPLICABLE

    Not able to be explained or interpreted

10. WSISH = 10. SWISH

    Move with a whistle or hiss

11. MPRVEIO = 11. IMPROVE

    Get better

12. IRUCREPOSA = 12. PRECARIOUS

    Dangerously lacking in security or stability

13. LAEDOEST = 13. DESOLATE

    Dreary; unfit for habitation or use

14. BNTHOIRGB = 14. THROBBING

    Beating rapidly or violently; pounding

15. ITNHCIHG = 15. HITCHING

    Hooking to; connecting

16. EVIONLTNIAT =16. VENTILATION

Admitting fresh air to replace stale air

17. RDEAVGEN =17. ENGRAVED

Carved, cut, or etched into something

18. LTLIAECM =18. METALLIC

Like or containing a metal

19. TUGVEFII =19. FUGITIVE

Person running away from the law

20. ENRTCA =20. NECTAR

Delicious, invigorating drink

21. NEMOV =21. VENOM

Poisonous secretion of an animal, such as a spider or snake

22. SNISTIS =22. INSISTS

Refuses to yield

23. LYULG =23. GULLY

Deep ditch cut in the earth by running water

24. OLTO =24. LOOT

Stolen goods

25. EAYLDED =25. DELAYED

Put off until another time

26. ZAHE =26. HAZE

Moisture, dust, or vapor suspended in the air

27. EVEDIRTER =27. RETRIEVED

Got back; regained

28. HFINCL =28. FLINCH

Draw away from something surprising or painful

29. EPEICRPCI =29. PRECIPICE

Extremely steep or overhanging mass of rock

VOCABLUARY JUGGLE LETTER 3 - Holes

1. IRAOT = 1. _____
   Relation between two things

2. IBLEECPADS = 2. _____
   Vile; awful

3. YIERF = 3. _____
   Very hot; like fire

4. FLINGTSI = 4. _____
   Smothering; suffocating

5. THGIANIIMLU = 5. _____
   Embarrassing; being disgraced

6. NREABR = 6. _____
   Sterile; dull; unfruitful

7. MIFARILA = 7. _____
   Often encountered; known

8. ORWEAERHWBL = 8. _____
   Vehicle with handles & a wheel used to convey loads by hand

9. ADEDR = 9. _____
   Anticipate with fear, alarm, or reluctance

10. FEITVDECE =10. _____
    Flawed; doesn't work right

11. TUBLES =11. _____
    So slight as to be difficult to distinguish

12. UEDSLALC =12. _____
    Having a thickening and hardness of skin

13. EUCPSST =13. _____
    Have doubts about; distrust

14. AMZADE =14. _____
    Filled with surprise; astonished

15. ONMCDEEND =15. _____
    Found guilty

16. RITDEWH   =16. _____
                          Twisted; squirmed

17. EUFEGR   =17. _____
                          Place of protection or shelter

18. NUISLAD   =18. _____
                          Instrument that indicates local solar time

19. RRQTMEEUINES   =19. _____
                          Necessary things

20. PTIEEAACPR   =20. _____
                          Value

21. OGYSG   =21. _____
                          Soaked with moisture

22. HASNRK   =22. _____
                          Got smaller

23. POICONSR   =23. _____
                          Spider-like animal with a venomous tail

24. GRAIME   =24. _____
                          An illusion; something deceptive

25. ITGOINITVSANE   =25. _____
                          Systematic examination

26. ACARCNTDERIE   =26. _____
                          Shut in; confined--usually in jail

27. ERHOV   =27. _____
                          Floating or suspended in air

28. ANDSETNCDES   =28. _____
                          Individuals from which others come; opposite of ancestors

29. OURGETEQS   =29. _____
                          Outlandish; bizarre

VOCABLUARY JUGGLE LETTER 3 ANSWER KEY - Holes

1. IRAOT = 1. RATIO
Relation between two things

2. IBLEECPADS = 2. DESPICABLE
Vile; awful

3. YIERF = 3. FIERY
Very hot; like fire

4. FLINGTSI = 4. STIFLING
Smothering; suffocating

5. THGIANIIMLU = 5. HUMILIATING
Embarrassing; being disgraced

6. NREABR = 6. BARREN
Sterile; dull; unfruitful

7. MIFARILA = 7. FAMILIAR
Often encountered; known

8. ORWEAERHWBL = 8. WHEELBARROW
Vehicle with handles & a wheel used to convey loads by hand

9. ADEDR = 9. DREAD
Anticipate with fear, alarm, or reluctance

10. FEITVDECE =10. DEFECTIVE
Flawed; doesn't work right

11. TUBLES =11. SUBTLE
So slight as to be difficult to distinguish

12. UEDSLALC =12. CALLUSED
Having a thickening and hardness of skin

13. EUCPSST =13. SUSPECT
Have doubts about; distrust

14. AMZADE =14. AMAZED
Filled with surprise; astonished

15. ONMCDEEND =15. CONDEMNED
Found guilty

16. RITDEWH	=16.	WRITHED
		Twisted; squirmed
17. EUFEGR	=17.	REFUGE
		Place of protection or shelter
18. NUISLAD	=18.	SUNDIAL
		Instrument that indicates local solar time
19. RRQTMEEUINES	=19.	REQUIREMENTS
		Necessary things
20. PTIEEAACPR	=20.	APPRECIATE
		Value
21. OGYSG	=21.	SOGGY
		Soaked with moisture
22. HASNRK	=22.	SHRANK
		Got smaller
23. POICONSR	=23.	SCORPION
		Spider-like animal with a venomous tail
24. GRAIME	=24.	MIRAGE
		An illusion; something deceptive
25. ITGOINITVSANE	=25.	INVESTIGATION
		Systematic examination
26. ACARCNTDERIE	=26.	INCARCERATED
		Shut in; confined--usually in jail
27. ERHOV	=27.	HOVER
		Floating or suspended in air
28. ANDSETNCDES	=28.	DESCENDANTS
		Individuals from which others come; opposite of ancestors
29. OURGETEQS	=29.	GROTESQUE
		Outlandish; bizarre

www.ingramcontent.com/pod-product-compliance
Lightning Source LLC
Chambersburg PA
CBHW051407070526
44584CB00023B/3322